T0326874

KNOWLEDGE, POWER, AND ACADEMIC FREEDOM

THE WELLEK LIBRARY LECTURES

The Wellek Library Lectures in Critical Theory are given annually at the University of California, Irvine, under the auspices of UCI Critical Theory. The following lectures were given in May 2008.

UCI CRITICAL THEORY

JAMES A. STEINTRAGER, DIRECTOR

For a complete list of Wellek Library Lectures see page 173.

KNOWLEDGE, POWER, AND ACADEMIC FREEDOM

JOAN WALLACH SCOTT

Columbia University Press *New York*

Columbia University Press
Publishers Since 1893
New York   Chichester, West Sussex
cup.columbia.edu

Copyright © 2019 Columbia University Press

Library of Congress Cataloging-in-Publication Data
Names: Scott, Joan Wallach, author.
Title: Knowledge, power, and academic freedom / Joan Wallach Scott.
Description: New York : Columbia University Press, [2019] |
Series: Wellek
Library lectures in critical theory | Includes
bibliographical references and index.
Identifiers: LCCN 2018026113| ISBN 9780231190466 (cloth : alk. paper) |
ISBN 9780231548939 (ebook)
Subjects: LCSH: Academic freedom—United States. | Learning and
scholarship—United States. | Higher education and state—United States. |
Education, Higher—Aims and objectives—United States.
Classification: LCC LC72.2 .S38 2019 | DDC 378.1/213—dc23
LC record available at https://lccn.loc.gov/2018026113

Columbia University Press books are printed on permanent
and durable acid-free paper.
Printed in the United States of America

Cover design: Lisa Hamm

CONTENTS

KNOWLEDGE, POWER, AND ACADEMIC FREEDOM

Introduction

ON THE FUTURE
OF ACADEMIC FREEDOM

These essays are variations on the theme of academic freedom. They return again and again to the founding documents of the principle, written in the heyday of the Progressive Era, the end of the nineteenth and the beginning of the twentieth centuries. Some of them cover similar ground from different perspectives because they were written for different occasions. They explore the tensions, paradoxes, and contradictions of the principle as well as its practical applications. And they are based on my reading of the many scholarly musings on its meaning as well as on my experience as a member of the Committee on Academic Freedom and Tenure of the American Association of University Professors (1993–2006 and 2013–2018). The essays are also avowedly political, invoking academic freedom in response to attacks on it and on the enterprise of higher education in the United States more generally. Some of the ideas in them were contained in the Wellek Library Lectures that I gave at the University of California, Irvine in 2008. I postponed publishing those lectures because I thought I needed time to think hard (and long) about the topic; as a result, this book arrives much later than anticipated. But I think history has been on my side—developments since 2008 have sharpened the stakes and raised issues I could not have addressed as fully at that time.

ACADEMIC FREEDOM UNDER FIRE

In my lifetime, academic freedom has been repeatedly under threat. In the 1950s, in the McCarthy era, hundreds of teachers were interrogated about their political beliefs and summarily fired, whether or not those beliefs had anything to do with the subject matter they taught.[1] In the 1990s "political correctness" was the term used by conservative critics of the university to attack the results of affirmative action and the subsequent increased diversity of students, faculty, and the curriculum. The first essay I wrote on the subject of academic freedom (chapter 1 in this volume) was for a series of lectures sponsored by the American Association of University Professors (AAUP) and subsequently published in 1996 in a book edited by Louis Menand. His introduction sought to reply to those who had denounced "multiculturalism" and "postmodernism" as philosophies that were antithetical to the truth-seeking project of the academy. He argued, as many of us did in our essays, that the presence of once-excluded groups in the university (women, African Americans, gays, and lesbians) required new forms of knowledge production; indeed, we pointed out that the supposed objectivity of an earlier curriculum was often a mask for entrenched patterns of discrimination. Challenges to disciplinary orthodoxies need not be violations of academic freedom, we insisted, but—when pursued with rigor and scholarly seriousness—were precisely exercises of that freedom.[2] The success of the new programs, and their widespread adoption, is testimony to the ways in which academic freedom can at once preserve the integrity of scholarship and enable dramatic expansion of what counts as legitimate knowledge. (Chapters 1 and 2 take up these issues.)

The question of academic freedom has come to the fore again in the early decades of the twenty-first century as right-wing groups have intensified their assaults on the university as a place of critical inquiry. Climate-change deniers go after climate scientists; antiabortion activists attack those engaged in stem-cell research; lobbyists for the State of Israel demand the dismissal of scholars in Middle Eastern Studies programs; and all manner of groups charge that interdisciplinary programs in women's, gender, sexuality, race, and ethnic studies are modes of indoctrination, not education. These attacks have been underwritten by a well-oiled propaganda machine, funded by right-wing individuals, foundations, and institutes (Heritage, Koch, Bradley, Amway, Goldwater) determined to discredit the critical thinking and intense debate long associated with a university education and to replace it with an exclusive emphasis on civility, conservative pedagogy, and vocational training. (See chapters 3 and 6.) The election of Donald Trump invigorated these groups and, with his anti-elitist, anti-intellectual, and white supremacist bias, gave political backing to them in the form of administrative orders and cabinet appointments. (For educators, the dismaying example is Trump's secretary of education, Betsy DeVos, whose family supports the Amway Foundation, a leading funder of attacks on public education at all levels, including the higher education "establishment.")

These groups are especially eager, as was Lynne Cheney when she headed the National Endowment for the Humanities (1986–1993), to protect a vision of national history that underplays, if it does not entirely ignore, slavery, racism, working-class and feminist protest, imperial outreach, economic inequality, and campaigns for social justice.[3] To further the attack on the academy, rightist foundations have funded online media sites such as the Professor Watchlist, which purports to identify dangerous left-wing professors and hopes to call their credentials into question, thereby ridding campuses of them. They have reduced critical scholarship to partisan politics, which is a different matter from what might be called the politics of academic knowledge—that is, debates about what counts as knowledge and how we determine it, including the way in which ethical commitments influence the things we study. Turning Point USA, which defines itself as "a youth organization that promotes the principles of fiscal responsibility, free markets, and limited government," has been given millions of dollars for its campus campaigns to elect conservative student governments and to secretly tape lectures and classroom discussions in the interest of "outing" the so-called leftists who control what its founder, Charlie Kirk, refers to as "islands of totalitarianism"—that is, existing college campuses.[4] Many of these deep-pocketed foundations led a concerted campaign during 2017 and 2018 to bring to campuses a succession of controversial speakers (few of them serious academics, most of them right-wing cable news commentators) who—astonishingly—sought to present white conservatives as victims of leftist intolerance. They have tested the limits of free speech on campus as far as possible and sought (sometimes successfully) to provoke the forms of resistance to their hate speech (calls for speaker bans, heckling, silencing of speakers, unruly demonstrations) that would provide evidence of their victimhood, leading to programs of "affirmative action" for conservatives! In the process, free speech and academic freedom have been invoked repeatedly, as if they were the same thing—they are not. (See chapter 6.)

WHAT IS ACADEMIC FREEDOM?

Academic freedom is an ideal, an aspiration. The South African literary scholar John Higgins refers to its definition as a "startling paradox" because "reference to it is usually motivated by its absence." "Academic freedom," he writes, "rarely if ever names, refers to or describes an existing state of things; rather it is always a normative ideal, called up precisely at moments when it is lacking or appears to be under threat."[5] Yet the ideal of academic freedom is crucial to our conception of the university. Menand calls it "the legitimating concept of the entire enterprise."[6] That said, he finds it "inherently problematic" because it is traversed by contradiction: free inquiry is essential to its definition, but it is inquiry patrolled and legitimated by disciplinary authority—a disciplinary authority that, in turn, warrants autonomy, the freedom of scholars from external pressure. The university provides knowledge essential to the operations of democracy, but knowledge production is not a democratic process because it rests on the expertise of researchers and teachers (chapter 2).

The university is not a marketplace of ideas in the sense that any opinion is worth hearing; it is, rather, a place in which "one voluntarily subjects one's own speech to the rules of some sort of 'truth procedure.'"[7] There is a difference, writes the legal scholar Adam Sitze, between "the pursuit of truth, on the one hand, and the unfettered exchange of opinions, on the other." "On these terms . . . ," he adds, "free inquiry in academia is predicated on voluntarily assumed forms of unfreedom that are unique to the academy."[8]

Academic freedom, then, is not about unfettered freedom of speech. It is at once a negative concept that calls for truth seeking by credentialed scholars free of interference from external powers (states, administrators, trustees, philanthropists, business interests, lobbyists, politicians, political activists). It is also a positive concept, insisting, in the words of the regents of the University of Wisconsin in 1894, that "whatever may be the limitations which trammel inquiry elsewhere, we believe that the great state University of Wisconsin should ever encourage that continual and fearless sifting and winnowing by which alone the truth can be found."[9]

Over the years since its articulation more than a century ago, the ideal has been debated and variously interpreted. Still, its general components can be named: autonomy of the university from state intervention; freedom of individual faculty to pursue research and to teach in their areas of expertise as well as the teacher's right—that of any citizen—to express political views outside the classroom; an accused faculty member's right to due process and to the judgment of his or her peers. These protections are granted academics as a self-regulating collectivity in recognition of their vital and unique contribution to "the common good," the prosperity, happiness, and general welfare of the nation as a whole. The legal scholars Matthew Finkin and Robert Post put it this way: "Academic freedom rests on a covenant struck between the university as an institution and the general public, not on a contract between particular scholars and the general public."[10] Distinguishing between individual rights and academic responsibility, they add: "If the First Amendment protects the interests of individual persons to speak as they wish, academic freedom protects the interests of society in having a professoriat that can accomplish its mission."[11]

The covenant Finkin and Post refer to dates to the Progressive Era, the moment of the establishment of major private and public research universities, their separation from sectarian religious influences, the professionalization of the professoriat, and the emergence of disciplinary societies. It rests on two assumptions. First is the assumption that higher education provides the nation with a *public good*, a set of benefits that advances not only the well-being of students but the nation as a whole. Critical advances in science, technology, social science, and the arts and humanities cannot be assessed in purely economic terms; they enrich the quality of the lives of the nation's people, even those who do not go to school. These benefits come from the production of knowledge, a process whose course cannot be predicted, whose effects are both long and short term. And—this is the second assumption—the process of the production of knowledge can only happen when the faculty is allowed to function as a self-regulating body.

The connection between higher education and the public, or common good, was articulated in the United States first in 1915 and elaborated in the 1940 "Statement on Principles on Academic Freedom and Tenure," a joint declaration of the AAUP and the Association of American Colleges.

> Institutions of higher education are conducted for the common good and not to further the interest of either the individual teacher or the institution as a whole. The common good depends upon the free search for truth and its free exposition. . . . Academic freedom can serve the public good only if universities as institutions are free from outside pressures in the realm of their academic mission and individual faculty members are free to pursue their research and teaching subject only to the academic judgment of their peers.[12]

This belief in the importance of higher education for promoting the common good is, in a sense, the infrastructure that has sustained the principle of academic freedom, its enduring utility (despite its many contradictions) over the years. Can the principle survive without that infrastructure? Has it lost its purchase in a new twenty-first century context?

THE UNIVERSITY IN RUINS?

In these essays I explore the concept of academic freedom and I argue for its continuing utility. But I also am worried about whether it can endure in the face not only of the presidency of Donald Trump and his Republican majority but of the long years of the devolution of higher education—a transformation that Bill Readings described as "the university in ruins" and that Chris Newfield refers to as "the great mistake."[13]

The transformation has taken place under Democratic and Republican administrations and at the national and state levels; it is as much an effect of the implantation of neoliberal capitalism as it is of party politics. In the realm of higher education, it has involved dramatically decreased public funding for colleges and universities; greater reliance on student tuition and a dramatic increase in student debt; greater need for private support, accompanied by increased intervention in academic decision-making by wealthy donors; the substitution of contingent employees for permanent, tenured faculty; a widening gap between richer and poorer institutions (one that parallels the widening gap between rich and poor in the population at large); the introduction of corporate management styles by academic administrators and boards of trustees and a consequent diminution of faculty participation in university governance; the substitution by university administrators of calculations of risk for evaluations of the quality of ideas; and the measurement of value of a university education exclusively in economic terms, as the enhancement of students' human capital instead of their cultural and intellectual resources. "Public higher education has undergone a financial and conceptual shift," writes the journalist Scott Carlson. "Once an investment covered mostly by the state to produce a workforce and an informed citizenry, today it is more commonly shouldered by individuals and families, and described as a private benefit, a means to a credential and a job."[14]

Wendy Brown, analyzing neoliberalism's reduction of all aspects of human life to economic calculation, describes its impact on higher education this way:

> Knowledge is not sought for purposes apart from capital enhancement, whether that capital is human, corporate, or financial. It is not sought for developing the capacities of citizens, sustaining culture, knowing the world, or envisioning and crafting different ways of life in common. Rather, it is sought for "positive ROI"— return on investment—one of the leading metrics the Obama administration propose[d] to use in rating colleges for would-be consumers of higher education.[15]

As knowledge has been instrumentalized in this way, so the vision of the common good has eroded as well. Brown notes that "when the domain of the political itself is rendered in economic terms, the foundation vanishes for citizenship concerned with public things and the common good. . . . The replacement of citizenship defined as concern with the public good by citizenship reduced to the citizen as *homo oeconomicus* also eliminates the very idea of a people, a demos asserting its collective political sovereignty."[16] Carlson points out the racist dimension to this. "As the student population has diversified, the language that many people use to define the value of a college degree has shifted, from a public good to an individual one. Is that merely a coincidence?"[17]

A heightened ideology of individualism and its concomitant practice of privatization have replaced belief in the common good—a belief on which the covenant between the university and the public good rested, and a belief that recognized academic freedom as an essential aspect of the agreement. Nothing symptomatizes this as clearly as the increasing tendency to treat academic freedom as synonymous with free speech and with the unfettered right of a student to his opinions in the classroom. The question of rights—defined as private properties belonging to individuals—has in turn overshadowed any discussion of the distinction between opinion and scholarship. In this view, everyone's opinion has equal weight, whatever their qualifications to justify it. Those who have pushed legislators to pass student bills of rights argue that the university is a "marketplace of ideas" in which all ideas are of equal value—the market will decide which is right or wrong. So any student has as much right to insist that creationism is a valid "theory" as his professor does to insist on evolution. So a professor whose teaching is critical of slavery is denounced as a racist by students who believe in defending white privilege. So students (right and left) dispute professorial teaching in the name of the authority of their personal experience. So a university insists that it cannot prevent a controversial speaker from advocating white nationalism or expressing misogynist ideas, even if his speech violates federal requirements that there be no hostile climate to undermine students' pursuit of education.[18]

The neoliberal privatizing ethos has undermined belief in a common good and, in consequence, eroded public faith in the mission of higher education. Increases in tuition and the enormous student debt that has ensued have alone led to charges of mismanagement and fraud, to the notion that universities are responsible for social inequality, and to the belief that academic freedom shelters elite professors from public accountability. These charges, encouraged by reactionary groups, are disturbingly widespread. And even when universities are proclaimed as furthering the national interest, it is an interest that is not defined in terms of public goods or collective well-being; rather, it is conceived as an open playing field on which there are winners and losers, judged according to their ability to accumulate and deploy their economic capital in their own interest. Donald Trump's campaign slogan, "Make America Great Again," was a promise to restrict that field to white Americans; his actions—to cut income taxes (the concrete embodiment of shared responsibility for our collective well-being) and so justify slashing spending on social services, health care, education, and environmental and consumer protection—will constitute a final blow to what was left of any commitment to or belief in the common good.

CRITICAL VOICES

Even as these changes occur, there has been important resistance to them. It has taken many forms—unionization of faculty, student protest, studies by educational associations, books and articles denouncing the loss of belief in what Finkin and Post call "the social good of advancing knowledge,"[19] and organizations that define their mission as promoting the continuing value of higher education (as we knew it) for the public good. Some of these efforts too easily buy into neoliberal economic logic, measuring the public good mainly in terms of returns to the state on its investment dollars.[20] Others emphasize the need to protect democracy and the importance of education in producing critical, discerning citizens.[21] The AAUP focuses on the protection of academic freedom itself as one of its primary preoccupations.

Some scholars have gone further, questioning whether academic freedom can exist in conditions of social inequality. So, for example, John Higgins asks (from the South African perspective, but with much broader implication) "What does the right to academic freedom mean in a society where the material foundations for its practice are lacking or unevenly distributed because of material inequalities?"[22] For him, the material foundations have to do with who has access to education and in what forms. The apartheid state granted a measure of autonomy to institutions that supported its policies, but not to the "open universities" that challenged them—to what extent could academic freedom be said to exist in that situation? In post-apartheid South Africa, is the differential availability of resources to support teaching and research an issue of academic freedom or something else? Are prohibitively high student fees an aspect of this freedom? What about segregation? Discrimination? Extending the question to Israel/Palestine, we might ask (as those of us protesting the occupation have) how the practices of the Israeli government have impeded Palestinian rights to academic freedom. Can academic freedom be said to exist in Israel if it is denied to Palestinians? How universal does the application of academic freedom have to be to be considered a valid operational practice? Who gets to count as a legitimate researcher in the unending pursuit of knowledge and truth? And what is the common good to which their thinking contributes?

These questions go beyond the scope of the essays in this book, but they deserve consideration. My response is that academic freedom is an ideal, an ethical aspiration (as I argue in chapter 1). There is value in protecting the ideal as an ideal—that's what makes it such a useful instrument. If there is a material aspect to it, it has to do with the autonomy of the faculty as a self-regulating body; without that practice, the ideal cannot be attained in any form. Beyond that, we can debate the varied implementations (or violations) of academic freedom as they occur; we can point to a climate (campus, state, national) that is favorable to it or not. We can expose the hypocrisy of its one-sided application, as in the Israeli case, even as we invoke it to condemn threats to the research and teaching of Israeli scholars. To defend academic freedom is to defend the production of knowledge—the pursuit of truth—as an open, unending process by a faculty "sifting and winnowing" its truth claims, always conducted with a certain discipline and rigor. Jonathan Cole puts it this way, "These . . . two components—tolerance for unsettling ideas and insistence on rigorous skepticism about all ideas— create an essential tension at the heart of the American research university. It will not thrive without both components operating effectively and simultaneously."[23] In a similar vein, Edward Said described intellectual discourse as "the freedom to be critical: criticism *is* intellectual life and, while the academic precinct contains a great deal in it, its spirit is intellectual and critical, and neither reverential nor patriotic."[24] (See chapter 5.)

But the defense of academic freedom also means the defense of the covenant on which it rests, a belief that there is something we conceive of as a public good and that that public good cannot do without critical thinking of the kind Cole and Said describe. Critical thinking, as John Dewey notes, is greatly resisted because it appears hostile to "habits and modes of life to which the people have accustomed themselves . . . and with which the worth of life is bound up."[25] But, he concludes, it was academic freedom that must protect critical thinkers from potential public wrath. The university has historically provided a shelter from that wrath; under its aegis, scholars should be permitted to produce the knowledge without which the common good would suffer irreparable harm. Academic freedom is precisely the privilege and the protection accorded to scholars to investigate the inequalities Higgins refers to and to propose more just social arrangements and the new forms of knowledge of which those arrangements are both cause and effect. It is the abstractness of the principle, and its embodiment in an autonomous faculty, that enables its varied uses and its concrete applications and that leaves it open to continuing interpretation and challenge. It is, in that way, one of the pillars of a democratic society, one we allow to crumble at our peril. When redefined as an individual right—a marketized free-for-all, no different from the right of free speech—academic freedom loses its purchase.

The fight for academic freedom, I argue, cannot take place on the grounds of that freedom alone; without some concept of the common good, as Dewey and his fellow Progressives articulated it, academic freedom will not survive. Those of us looking to (re)articulate some notion of a common good need academic freedom to protect the spaces of our critical inquiry. In turn, the survival of the concept of academic freedom depends on our ability to come up with that rearticulation. The future of the common good and of academic freedom are bound up together. The one will not survive without the other.

1

ACADEMIC FREEDOM AS AN ETHICAL PRACTICE

Fairly early in my life I began to learn about academic freedom. It was a complicated lesson. In my family, academic freedom was an unquestioned ideal, a matter of principle invoked repeatedly throughout the difficult years of the 1950s and early 1960s. At the same time, I had good reason to be skeptical of the power of the ideal, for I knew that it could be violated in practice. My father was a New York City high school teacher, suspended in 1951 (when I was ten) and fired in 1953 for refusing to cooperate first with a congressional committee and then with the superintendent of schools on their investigations into communist activity among teachers. Although formally tenured according to the rules of the board of education, my father lost his job because, in that moment of the early Cold War, his refusal to discuss his political beliefs and affiliations was taken as evidence that he was a communist and therefore unfit to teach: This despite the fact that he was a devoted fan of Thomas Jefferson, the Bill of Rights, and the Constitution, and that his students and their parents testified to the ways in which his history classes deepened their appreciation of American democracy.

In the tallying of losses he experienced in that period—his job, his pension, his financial security, many colleagues he had once considered friends—none was so painful as the loss of his academic freedom. At the same time, the existence of the principle was something he could hold on to, a right that was still his and to which he could appeal. I remember wondering why he cared so much about a principle that had failed to protect him from an arbitrary exercise of political power, but I also understood that the principle had some tangible existence for him independent of its ability to bring about the effects it was designed to secure.

Writing in 1955, Fritz Machlup, then of Johns Hopkins University, argued that academic freedom became a reality only when some scholars, having been accused of "abusing" their academic freedom, were nonetheless protected from those seeking to punish them for their presumed offenses. "When these pressures and temptations to interfere are resisted and the offenders are assured of their immunity, then, and only then, is academic freedom shown to be a reality. Thus, the occurrences of so-called abuses of academic freedom, far from being incompatible with the existence of academic freedom, are the only proofs of its existence."[1] In my father's case, the situation was the reverse: having failed to protect him from "these pressures and temptations to interfere," academic freedom existed nonetheless. Indeed, it was precisely in its loss that the abstract principle acquired concrete reality. And it was in the name of the defense of and subsequent pursuit of this lost object that my father justified his "insubordinate" behavior at the board of education and sustained his moral outrage and sense of righteous indignation at the betrayal represented by his treatment (and that of the some-350 other New York City school teachers who were forced out in those years). I can now say that academic freedom functioned as an "ethics" for my father, in the way Michel de Certeau has defined it. "Ethics," he writes, "is articulated through effective operations, and it defines a distance between what is and what ought to be. The distance designates a space where we have something to do."[2]

One of the confusing things about "academic freedom" for me in that period was that there was more than one meaning—indeed, there were contradictory meanings—to be found for the term. My father understood academic freedom as an individual teacher's or scholar's right not to be judged by any criteria but the quality of his teaching or scholarship. Others thought that academic freedom pertained only to the actual pursuit of scholarly inquiry, protecting from outside interference only those who actually espoused unpopular or unorthodox views in writing or in the classroom. The board of education had yet another definition. It sometimes argued that in order to protect the autonomy of the teaching establishment from "outside" interference, it had to clean its own house by purging politically suspect teachers. In this definition, the greater good of the profession required the sacrifice of its most unconventional or troublesome members. All sides in this confrontation insisted that academic freedom had only one meaning and that meaning was absolute.

In fact, I think the concept of academic freedom carries many meanings (the defense of individual rights of inquiry, of unpopular ideas, and corporate autonomy), and these meanings are (and have been) developed differently in different relationships of power and in different historical circumstances. Although in 1951 my vocabulary didn't include the notion either of paradox or ambiguity, I think they are what I was observing. Academic freedom, like any notion of freedom or rights, is (in the words of political theorist Wendy Brown) "neither a philosophical absolute nor a tangible entity, but a relational and contextual practice that takes shape in opposition to whatever is locally and ideologically conceived as unfreedom."[3] At the same time, its idiom is necessarily ahistorical and acontextual; indeed, it is precisely because "academic freedom" is thought to stand outside specific political contexts, as a universal principle, that it can be invoked as a check on specific abuses of power. This tension between academic freedom as a historically circumscribed relationship and an enduring universal ideal cannot be resolved; it is what gives the concept its ethical and practical force. The effort to resolve the tension by insisting on the one true definition is to engage in an exercise of dogmatism that can only disarm the concept it purports to defend. By dogmatism I mean the claim to be authorized by some immutable truth that can entertain no legitimate objection to itself and then to impose laws—to determine inclusions and exclusions—in the name of that truth.[4]

To acknowledge the inherent internal contradiction and the historical variability of a principle is not to give up on the possibility of making judgments. I have no difficulty condemning the board of education's actions, and not only because my father's dismissal profoundly affected my life. My condemnation is an interpretation of a set of circumstances in which, it seems to me, political hysteria substituted for reasoned action, no evidence of subversive activity—in or outside the classroom—was ever produced, and those most in need of protection (the political dissenters) were systematically denied it. When weighed against the harm done to an individual in this instance, arguments for the protection of corporate autonomy seem weak, if not beside the point (though I concede that, in other instances, different conclusions might be drawn). The point is that, although academic freedom is a principle, its content is never clear-cut. Specific cases are always complex and, as those of us who sit through the long meetings of Committee A (the American Association of University Professors committee charged with investigating violations of academic freedom) learn firsthand, they always involve contestation: differences of interpretation and therefore debate about what has happened and why. It is the debate about cases (and provisional agreement that allows for adjudication) that articulates historical meanings for academic freedom. This debate is the "effective operation" that takes place in the space "between what is and what ought to be" and so constitutes another example of what de Certeau means by "ethics."

EARLY DEFINITIONS

If, as I have argued, the power of academic freedom lies precisely in the ambiguity of its existence as a universal principle and as a historically circumscribed relationship—in the distance between what ought to be and what is—and if dogmatism is the great threat to academic freedom because it seeks to banish ambiguity by appealing to absolute truth, we are not rid of the threat for having pointed it out. For the problem of dogmatism is not external to academic freedom but is another of those ambiguities at the very heart of the concept. Academic freedom protects those whose thinking challenges orthodoxy; at the same time, the legitimacy of the challenge—the proof that the critic is not a madman or a crank—is secured by membership in a disciplinary community based upon shared commitment to certain methods, standards, and beliefs. While that commitment doesn't force agreement at every level of practice, it does resist assaults on its fundamental premises (in my field, a reflexive acceptance of a certain notion of "history" as the empirical object of study) and in this way functions as orthodoxy. The critic of orthodoxy thus, ironically, must find legitimation in the very discipline whose orthodoxy he or she challenges.

Let me illustrate this point a bit more. Academic freedom has meant protection for the critical function of scholars and teachers who believed they were attempting to advance knowledge by calling into question widely held or accepted beliefs. This questioning, moreover, is not trivial or superficial, it is fundamental. It introduces ideas that are "unassimilable," that cannot be integrated into a prevailing corpus.[5] While Galileo was the archetypical example of this kind of unassimilable idea in the narrative of scientific progress, twentieth-century commentators worried more about protecting the expression of scholars in fields that could not make a full claim to scientific standing. Thus, John Dewey, in his remarkably prescient (from our end-of-the-century perspective) 1902 essay "Academic Freedom," pointed to the lower scientific status of "the social and psychological disciplines and to some phases of linguistic and historical study—those most intimately associated with religious history and literature."[6] Scholars in these fields need "the utmost freedom of investigation," he suggests, because they deal more closely than technical scientists with "the problems of life," and are thus more likely to come up against deep-rooted prejudice and intense emotional reaction: "These exist because of the habits and modes of life to which the people have accustomed themselves. To attack them is to appear to be hostile to institutions in which the worth of life is bound up."[7]

Dewey asserts, on the one hand, that academic freedom would result in the "advance" of these fields, but he also recognizes, on the other hand, that they might remain "partial sciences," lacking the detachment and technical mastery that at once guaranteed popular acceptance of the authority of physics and chemistry and confined those fields to "problems of technical theory." (Because of debates about evolution, biology was still in a "transitional" state.) The urgency of social needs could not be met by technicians; Dewey thought that specialization, however scientific its allure, meant withdrawal from "the larger issues of life."[8] It was a kind of privatization, the opposite of public action. To the mastery of science, Dewey counterposes the "virility" of social engagement. (Here masculinity marked public as opposed to private action.) Specialization, he insists, posed an "immediate danger to courage, and the freedom that can only come from courage."[9]

> Teaching: in any case, is something of a protected industry; it is sheltered. The teacher is set somewhat one side [sic] from the incidence of the most violent stresses and strains of life. His problems are largely intellectual, not moral; his associates are largely immature. There is always the danger of a teacher's losing something of the virility that comes from having to face and wrestle with economic and political problems on equal terms with competitors. Specialization unfortunately increases these dangers. It leads the individual, if he follows it unreservedly, into bypaths still further off from the highway where men, struggling together, develop strength. The insidious conviction that certain matters of fundamental import to humanity are none of my concern because outside of my *Fach*, is likely to work more harm to genuine freedom of academic work than any fancied dread of interference from a moneyed benefactor.[10]

The ideas that underlay men's virile struggles with economic and political problems could not claim the same kind of objectivity that technical science did. For this reason, Dewey suggests that "the problem of academic freedom becomes to a very large extent a personal matter," involving the "style" and "manner" of an individual's presentation—things that could not easily be regulated and were, moreover, not necessarily an indicator of the seriousness of a scholar's teaching.

> Whenever scientific method is only partially attained the danger of undue dogmatism and of partisanship is very great. It is possible

to consecrate ideas born of sheer partisanship with the halo of scientifically established belief. It is possible to state what is currently recognized to be scientific truth in such a way as to violate the most sacred beliefs of a large number of our fellow men. The manner of conveying the truth may cause an irritation quite foreign to its own substance. This is quite likely to be the case whenever the negative rather than the positive aspect is dwelt upon; wherever the discrepancy between the new truth and established institutions is emphasized, rather than the intrinsic significance of the new conception. The outcome is disintegrating instead of constructive; and the methods inevitably breed distrust and antagonism.[11]

If polemic could be disguised as science, and science mistaken for partisanship, on what basis could the reliability of a professor's pronouncements be ascertained? Dewey cites University of Chicago president William Rainey Harper's 1900 convocation address as an answer. In addition to refraining from sensationalism and political partisanship in the classroom, Harper insisted that scholars restrict their expressions to their areas of competence and refrain from promulgating as truth "ideas or opinions which have not been tested scientifically by . . . colleagues in the same department of research or investigation."[12] This notion of a disciplinary community of researchers held great promise for Dewey, and he came back to it at the end of his essay. Such a community, he thought, would "solidify and reinforce otherwise scattered and casual efforts" of individual scholars and give them the courage to resist pressures internal to the university that dampened the autonomy needed for the pursuit of truth. Disciplinary communities (Dewey called them "scientific associations") were the guarantee of both the independence of the individual scholar in an increasingly centralized and oligarchic university and the integrity of his work. They were "an imme-diate resource counteracting the dangers threatening academic freedom."[13]

For Dewey, as for later commentators, the disciplinary com-munity provided support for the individual, verifying his or her technical expertise and qualifications. Indeed, it was that communal self-regulation based in a certain expertise that made academic freedom different from other notions of individual rights. But there was little acknowledgment that there was also a tension between the regulatory authority of a disciplinary community and the autonomy of its individual members, that discipline was necessarily exclusionary, and that this might mean scholarly critique could be threatened from within. "Cor-porate scientific consciousness" Dewey defines glowingly as "the sense of the solidarity of truth. Whatever wounds the code of truth in one of its members attacks the whole organism."[14] Defining "academic freedom" in the 1937 edition of the *Encyclo-pedia of the Social Sciences*, Arthur Lovejoy also stresses the advan-tages for an individual scholar of subsumption in a disciplinary community. The individual scholar, he points out, checked by "qualified bodies of his own profession," is enabled to stand up against outside interference from "political or ecclesiastical authority, or from the administrative officials of the institution in which he is employed."[15] In the 1968 edition of the· *Interna-tional Encyclopedia of the Social Sciences*, Glenn Morrow develops the idea even further. The condition for the advance of knowl-edge, he writes, rests on the impossibility of ever finally estab-lishing the truth of a truth claim.

> Even after prolonged examination and testing, the claim can be accorded only a high degree of probability; and its status is never immune to later criticism. These conditions imply a community

of scholars and scientists cooperating with one another through mutual criticism and selecting and recruiting new members through disciplined and systematic training. These very requirements tended to produce such a community, animated by a professional spirit and resentful of any attempts by incompetent outside authorities to control its activities or judge its results.[16]

Here academic freedom rests on the protection afforded individuals by their disciplines against "incompetent outside authorities." What is ignored is the possible conflict between "mutual criticism" and the selection of new members "through disciplined and systematic training." Morrow, like Dewey, makes the correction of error, argument about interpretation, and the "approval and disapproval" of peers an entirely positive dimension of scholarly activity. But the inseparable other side of that regulatory and enabling authority is that it secures consensus by exclusion. And the grounds for exclusion can be, historically have been, *difference*—difference from some representative type (John Dewey's "virile"—and I would add white—male, for example, as the prototypical social scientist or humanist) or difference from the reigning philosophical and methodological assumptions (about causality, say, or intentionality, or the transparency of fact in the writing of history).

The ambiguity of discipline is unavoidable: the institution of the discipline, which protects the academic freedom of individuals, also operates to deny some of them that freedom. Put in other terms, discipline is at once productive (it permits the organization of knowledge and it authorizes the knowledge producer) and confining (it installs explicit and tacit normative standards that, when they are understood to be provisional, can serve important mediating functions but that, when they are taken as dogmatic precepts, become instruments of punishment).

The two aspects cannot be disentangled; discipline functions in a necessarily paradoxical way.

That freedom and subjection are two sides of the same coin is not a new insight, but it bears repeating at a time when the whole issue of disciplinarity has been thrown open to question by epistemological challenges to disciplinary foundations and by debates about the politics of knowledge and the relationship between the pursuit of knowledge and contemporary political concerns. These debates date at least to the 1960s, a time of enormous expansion of universities, the beginning of the diversification of their faculties and student bodies, and the politicization of university life by the Vietnam War. In that context, the question of the "relevance" of disciplinary authority was repeatedly posed. I remember long arguments with fellow graduate students at the University of Wisconsin about whether "history from the bottom up" was the only socially responsible history to write and about whether, indeed, one could justify one's desire for graduate training at all.[17] In the end, most of us got degrees and became university teachers, accepting the need for discipline even as we hoped to make our history more relevant by overturning canonical teachings and exposing their (conservative) foundational premises. Without discipline, there was no way to articulate the problematics that concerned us, no historical frame within which to pose our questions and search for answers, no structure in terms of which (and against which) fundamental critical challenges could be posed. Disciplines carried with them a whole intellectual history of contest about the legitimacy of questions and the frameworks for answering them and so provided the conditions of possibility for their own critical transformation. They also provided the conditions of possibility for interdisciplinarity—at its best, the use of articulated structures of inquiry to address problems in new or different domains.

THE CONFLICTS OF
THE CULTURE WARS

If there was a more intense "crisis" in the 1980s and 1990s than when I was a graduate student in the 1960s, it had to do with the suppression of the intellectual history of disciplines (and their portrayal as increasingly refined techniques or methodologies) and the attempt to resolve the necessary tension between discipline and critical challenge by forcing a choice between them. The extreme polarization of opinion about the role disciplines ought to play in the organization of academic knowledge was everywhere apparent: in the debates about the status of canonical and noncanonical texts, about the truth of competing historical narratives, about the relevance of the standpoint or identity or personal experience of the speaker to the authority of his or her knowledge, about the relationship between freedom of expression and the exercise of power, about the place of interdisciplinary programs in the curriculum, and about the uses and abuses of scholarly authority (including its erotic aspects) for classroom pedagogy.[18] Discipline usually figured in these debates either as that which must be restored in its most dogmatic form—foundational assumptions are taken to have fixed, enduring, and inherent value—or as that which must be exposed as the mask of oppressive power and replaced by a more emancipatory politics whose authority is based in personal experience. Discipline was either fetishized as immutable or rejected as an instrument of repression.

In this polarized atmosphere there was no middle ground; that is the reason the "culture wars" metaphor was so apt. The positions were not only entrenched and mutually exclusive, making reconciliation or persuasion impossible, they were also characterized by intense moralism. Moralism is an expression of resentment and anger; it is hope gone sour and analysis that has lost its bearings. It individualizes social problems, blaming those who would point them out for having caused them in the first place. And moralism, as Wendy Brown has so skillfully described it, "tends to be intensely antagonistic toward . . . a richly agonistic political or intellectual life. . . . The identity of the moralist is . . . staked against intellectual inquiry which might tear up the foundations of its own premises; its survival is imperiled by the very practice of open-ended intellectual inquiry."[19] As moralism gains the day, so does dogmatism, and the basis for academic freedom is seriously undermined. This is because dogmatism insists that its truths are immune to criticism or change. Dogmatism denies the need that scholars have to pursue a logic of inquiry wherever it might lead.

As examples, there was, on the one hand, the furious assault on—indeed, the demonization of—those challenging disciplinary premises as "postmodernists."[20] As if postmodernists were the cause of all the problems of disciplinary uncertainty scholars were now facing; as if their banishment could end the questions about difference posed by demographic changes in university populations, by the emergence of postcolonial critiques of colonial assumptions, by developments in the history of philosophy that reached back to at least the nineteenth century, by the more recent end of the Cold War, and by the extraordinary economic constraints of those last years. The attack on so-called postmodernists as Nazi sympathizers, communists, nihilists, and moral relativists was revealing for the way in which it politicized contests about knowledge. It made the presumed political implications of one's scholarly ideas, not the ideas themselves, the ultimate ground for exclusion. The deflection of the issue not only offered a political test for what was being defended as objective knowledge, it also precluded serious discussion of the more difficult philosophical matters at stake. This refusal to engage serious philosophical critique, moreover, played into anti-intellectual currents in society at large and thus into the hands of those attacking the university from outside (whether the attacks came in the form of congressional scrutiny or massive defunding).

The virulent attack being waged on postmodernists is only one example of the way upholders of orthodoxy sought to bar from the field critics of foundational disciplinary premises. By denying these critics the legitimacy that disciplinary membership confers, such attacks precluded claims by them that their academic freedom had been violated. Ironically, the tables were sometimes turned as the defenders of orthodoxy invoked the protection of academic freedom against internal critics as if the critics were outsiders, effectively banishing them. (In one instance, a conservative author who received a negative book review claimed that her academic freedom had been violated by the reviewer, depicted as an outsider, who was in fact a scholar with expertise on the subject matter of the book but who held a different political position from her own.[21]) The point is, boundaries of inclusion and exclusion were being rigidly drawn, not only to deal with current critics but to warn future generations of the high price of apostasy. It was dogmatism in action.

On the other hand, critics of orthodoxy blamed the mistreatment of minorities both in the curriculum and in the society at large on the oppressive influence of disciplinary authority. Thus, in an article in the *Chronicle of Higher Education*, a white literary critic, replying to charges by African American women that her color disqualified her from writing about novels like Toni Morrison's *Beloved*, argues that it was not color that was the problem but the disciplinary training that had supplied her with "the tricks of textual mastery." By attempting to "master" texts with rigorous theoretical analyses "constructed by white male critics," she thought women such as herself were unthinkingly reenacting the subjugation and the oppressive domination of blacks by whites. As an alternative, she urges white women to disavow "mastery" and write about their emotional responses to the text. The goal, she argues, ought to be to "focus more on pondering the way our historical, cultural, and personal identities connect" with stories such as *Beloved*. This "pondering" happens best, she insists, without external direction; in this way personal emotional experience substituted for disciplinary authority.[22] From this vantage point, the practice as well as the purpose of reading texts is reduced to a process of self-discovery that not only contradicts the author's stated political aim of understanding and respecting difference but also forecloses the need for education, conceived as the training of minds and the imparting of new knowledge to them. In place of her disciplinary expertise, the teacher has the certainty of her political beliefs. What authority she has in her classroom rests on her dogmatic assertion of those beliefs and her expectation that they ought to be shared by her students. When that is not the case, there is no protection from the charge that she is "silencing" the opinions of some of her dissenting students, no way to prove that her criticisms of their work have not denied them freedom of speech. The invocation of "academic freedom" in what may be speech cases, but certainly are not academic freedom cases (as when students claim violation of *their* academic freedom because the teacher disagreed with their opinions), testify to the weakening, if not the disappearance, of the idea of disciplinary legitimation for classroom pedagogy.

Despite their opposition to one another, these two examples (the attack on postmodernism and the attack on disciplinarity) both represent attempts to build community—in one case a disciplinary community, in the other a political community—on a foundation of immutable truth.[23] The proponents of disciplinary orthodoxy take for granted the enduring value—the fixed truth—of their discipline's current epistemological foundations. For historians, this is the idea that history is an empirical object that could be studied more or less objectively. Interpretation of specific events such as the French Revolution might vary, as might attributions of causality, but consensus about the existence of "history" as a discoverable sequence of events with a correct interpretation is taken to be the ground of membership in the community of historians. Some historians, otherwise students of ineluctable change, inconsistently resist the idea that this concept of history could change (although, as the intellectual history of the field shows, it has in the past). They prophesize anarchy as the very least of the consequences that would follow from even engaging with philosophical critiques of "history." Israel, to paraphrase Peter Novick's anguished cry, will lose its king.[24]

An important strain of opposition to disciplinarity bases its community on the shared belief that knowledge is instrumental politics.[25] This is a very different position from the one that says that there is a politics (a set of historically specific institutional, ideological, and personal contests) necessarily associated with the production of knowledge. The instrumentalist view is far more reductive, conflating the politics of knowledge with politics in general, so that, for example, an expansion of the literary canon is seen as a direct political empowerment of previously excluded persons, or the overthrow of the idea of objectivity is seen as crucial to the advancement of women. Although literary canons and strong claims to objectivity may indeed be related to the entrenchment of white male privilege, it is not at all clear that there is a direct relationship between them. At the very least, the histories of canons and of objectivity are also disciplinary histories that cannot be reduced to simple morality tales about power and politics. When they are, when there is assumed to be a one-to-one correspondence between thought and its political impact, scholarly differences are inevitably taken to be political differences; those who think this is not the case are considered naive or complicit, enemies because they stand outside the consensus on which the community of righteousness must be based.[26]

In the standoff between these two communities, the functions of discipline and criticism are separated from one another; the one is reduced to dogmatic policing of standards and norms, the other limited to political advocacy. Their interaction is precluded, even as the existence of each is predicated on the exclusion of the other. And yet it is precisely the interaction of discipline and criticism—the necessary contests between them—that, ideally, academic freedom mediates and that defines academic freedom as an ethical practice.

ACADEMIC FREEDOM IN PRACTICE

Since disciplines are often referred to as "communities of the competent," it is worthwhile trying to think about the two terms—discipline and community—together, specifically about whether the dogmatic form I describe is the only one available. I don't think it is, but I also think elaborating an alternative requires something more than pious nods to pluralism and tolerance.

Communities assume some kind of consensus and thus are necessarily exclusionary; discipline separates the trained from the untrained. Disciplinary communities consist of people who agree to follow a certain set of rules in order to be trained. The key to thinking about nonorthodox disciplinary communities may lie not in the abandonment of these rules but in the clarification of how the rules are conceived: whether they are considered immutable, whether they are thought to implement a set of fixed beliefs, whether they countenance the kinds of contests that would lead to their own transformation.

If we think of communities and disciplines not as common essences, not as bodies of people who are the same (whether that sameness comes from shared identity or from shared belief in metaphysical truth), but as provisional entities called into being to organize relations of difference, then standards and rules become heuristic practices around which argument is expected and change anticipated.[27] What disciplinary communities share, in this view of them, is a common commitment to the autonomous pursuit of knowledge and a common agreement that such pursuit requires regulation. It might be better to say here that what is pursued is not truth or even knowledge (both of which imply some settled package of uncontestable information) but understanding (which retains the notion that there is something to be known that is apart from the scholar, and at the same time conveys the idea that interpretation always structures what is known).[28]

Disciplinary communities, then, share a common commitment to the autonomous pursuit of understanding, which they both limit and make possible by articulating, contesting, and revising the rules of such pursuits and the standards by which outcomes will be judged. (Understanding, after all, requires the same rigor and must be subjected to the same evaluation as knowledge; it is not based entirely on empathy or experience.) The problem of exclusion doesn't disappear from this more provisional notion of a disciplinary community, but its functional and arbitrary nature are clearly recognized. This recognition insists on a place for criticism and critical transformation at the very heart of the conception of a discipline and so guarantees the existence of that scholarly critical function that discipline is meant to legitimate and that academic freedom is designed to protect.

But what is the practical relationship of academic freedom to this conception of a discipline? Can academic freedom protect from the tendency to orthodoxy within a discipline the critical function on which it most depends? What role does a claim of academic freedom have in mediating relations between defenders and critics of orthodoxy on matters of the quality of work or the granting of tenure? Is academic freedom useful only as a protection against interference from outside the discipline, from government agencies, trustees, administrators, affirmative action officers, and sexual harassment counselors? Or can it be deployed to settle intradisciplinary conflicts? The answers are difficult and not clear-cut, intensifying the sense of crisis occasioned by the tendency to equate discipline with orthodoxy and criticism with politics.

A look at AAUP Committee A's deliberations provides illustration of these difficulties. The committee is on record as having rejected the idea that belief in the governing principles of a profession or discipline ought to be a condition of employment. In 1985 it stated clearly that academic freedom must protect even those deemed "nihilists" by their colleagues for their skepticism about the very foundations of the discipline.[29]

As a statement of principle, the 1985 report suggests broad scope for academic freedom in mediating disciplinary disputes. But, in practice, Committee A didn't treat all exercises or even abuses of disciplinary power (the granting of tenure, for example, or the decision to substitute one methodological or interpretive approach for another, or the phasing in or out of whole areas of study) as violations of academic freedom. This was because such intervention would bring questions of individual scholarly rights into arenas where they do not belong, arenas where the collective political battles that implement and challenge hierarchy, and so effect disciplinary change, must be waged. Even though these are exactly the battles that may constitute (racial, gender, ethnic, religious, epistemological) difference as an implicit ground for hierarchy, and in that way limit a scholar's freedom, they cannot be said to violate academic freedom. To analyze disciplinary power only in terms of academic freedom is to reduce complex structural and intellectual processes (that must be analyzed and engaged with as such) to questions of individual rights. One may impinge on the other, but they cannot be addressed or remedied in the same way. So, paradoxically, if academic freedom is to remain an effective protection for individual critical scholarly inquiry, it cannot be invoked in most of the battles about the rules and standards that underwrite the individual scholar's open-ended pursuit of understanding. In the collective process that articulates disciplinary power, academic freedom is not usually the most appropriate intervention.

And yet, of course, there are always the gray areas that must be interpreted, that cannot be decided in advance (the negative tenure case that does violate academic freedom, for example). For that reason, it seems to me, academic freedom must include substantive judgments, not just procedural judgments. Academic freedom is committed to an ideal of the unfettered pursuit of understanding that exists beyond structures of inequality or domination, yet it always addresses concrete situations (within disciplines and between scholars and "outsiders") that involve difference and power. At its best, academic freedom doesn't simply monitor such situations for the exercise of due process (although due process is a necessary condition for the unfettered pursuit of understanding) but intervenes to point out the ways in which certain (but not all) of the practices that enforce exclusions interfere with an individual's ability to pursue his or her inquiry wherever it leads. The adjudicatory function of academic freedom is to decide, in the context of specific cases, which are and which aren't violations. By imagining autonomy to be an individual right, academic freedom attempts to negotiate the necessarily relational and conflictual nature of the actual pursuit of understanding. Strategically, academic freedom endorses an ideal of scholarly activity that is blind to power in order to be able to see how power is abused in particular cases and whether those abuses constitute violations of academic freedom. Blindness and insight are thus crucially interdependent, enabling the kind of critical specificity that separates ethics from dogma.

Academic freedom lives in the ethical space between an ideal of the autonomous pursuit of understanding and the specific historical, institutional, and political realities that limit such pursuits. Its existence recognizes the complexity and necessary conflict that inhere in the activities of so-called truth seekers, and in the dangers that follow from consolidation around any particular truth (including an idea of truth itself). Academic freedom can never be boiled down to an essence; it is instead an ethical practice aimed not only at the protection of individuals but at (what Dewey and his associates thought of as) the advancement of our collective well-being.

In the late twentieth, and now in the twenty-first century, cynicism seems to have become the national ethos, a result at least in part of the loss of belief in the master narrative of progress that once sustained my father in his principled refusal to compromise his rights.[30] One symptom of this loss is, I suggest, an enormous outpouring of nostalgia for the substantive values of family, decency, "standards of excellence," morality, commonality, and truth. The cure for the seemingly insoluble problems of the present is thought to be a return to a past in which meanings were self-evident and universally shared, a past, in other words, that is dogmatically conceived.

The problems we confront are tremendously difficult: an increasing imbalance in the distribution of economic resources nationally and globally, an increasing impotency of citizens in the political sphere, an inability to negotiate the seemingly irreducible differences among contending groups in the society. But the answer does not consist in the infusion of "values" into the national psyche. Along that path lies the elimination of enemies and the enforcement of orthodoxy, the end of history and the final solution. The insistence on a return to "values" precludes precisely what is probably the only answer we have: a notion of ethical practice. While "values" represent closed meanings, "ethical practice" is an operation open to change. In de Certeau's definition with which I began this essay, the effective operation of ethics "defines a distance between what is and what ought to be. This distance designates a space where we have something to do." That distance is the open space of history. Not the history of grand teleological promises but the history that inscribes time as the embodiment of changing human relationships, changing in relation to a changing set of ideals that are as elusive in practice as they are practical in their effects.

It may be self-serving, or at least entirely predictable, for a historian to offer history as the best way to think about academic freedom. But that is what I want to do. I will be forgiven, perhaps, if I say I am not offering prevailing professional sentiment but that I speak as a critic embattled within her own field.

Academic freedom is a tense mediation of relationships, an imperfect contest about issues that can never be totally resolved. As such, it is a commitment to time and to history. With it, we are not always spared the punishment that orthodoxy metes out to its critics; without it, the critical function of scholarship and the possibility it represents for change would be lost. Academic freedom, then, is both a guarantor and an exemplification of the ethical practice that constitutes history, the relentless striving to close the distance between what is and what ought to be.

2

KNOWLEDGE, POWER, AND ACADEMIC FREEDOM

Although the term "academic freedom" has come to seem self-evident—so often is it invoked to condemn egregious violations of the perceived rights of members of university communities—it is, in fact, a complicated idea with limited application. In its origins in the United States at the turn of the last century, academic freedom pertained only to faculty—to those who produced and transmitted the knowledge necessary for the advancement of the common good. And not necessarily to tenured faculty, since the practice was virtually unknown then. Academic freedom was aimed at resolving conflicts about the relationships between power and knowledge, politics and truth, action and thought by positing sharp distinctions between them, distinctions that have been difficult to maintain. Rather than offer a pat definition, I want to look at some of the tensions that bedevil the concept of academic freedom, both as a theory of faculty rights and as a practice that can defend them.

THE BUSINESS OF THE UNIVERSITY

The American version of the doctrine of academic freedom, codified in the 1915 "Declaration of Principles" of the American

Association of University Professors (AAUP), was formulated during the Progressive Era at a crucial moment in the history of higher education, one that saw the coming into prominence of the research university.[1] The idea of academic freedom was premised not only on a sharp distinction between religious and secular institutions but also on the autonomy of the faculty of the new research university from the very forces that supported it: state legislatures and philanthropic businessmen. If the tension between what John Dewey referred to as sectarian discipleship and intellectual discipline seemed relatively easy to resolve (by the time of the AAUP's declaration, colleges were no longer exclusively training grounds for the ministry), the antagonism between corporate America and the American university persists to this day. As early as 1902 (in an essay called "Academic Freedom"), Dewey warned of the erosion of the educational mission by the need to curry favor with funders: "The great event in the history of an institution is now likely to be a big gift rather than a new investigation or the development of a strong and vigorous teacher."[2]

Dewey was not alone in his worry about the effects of money on the production of knowledge. Thorstein Veblen's trenchant critique of the business methods of universities, *The Higher Learning in America*, was published in 1916, followed in 1923 by Upton Sinclair's denunciation of the close ties between corporate America and universities: *The Goose-Step: A Study in American Education*. The passion and polemical tone of these books attest to the intensity of the conflict as it was felt in those years. These authors were responding to pressure from financial backers such as Clarence Birdseye, a lawyer and the father of the future frozen food magnate, who, in 1907, compared "college standards" unfavorably with "business principles." He urged faculty and administrators to imitate "a good manufacturer," and alumni to "help

introduce business methods into the work of your alma mater."
Andrew Carnegie had no use for humanistic training, arguing
that it was "fatal" to "the future captain of industry." And Fred-
erick Winslow Taylor offered models of corporate efficiency for
the reorganization of university life.[3] Businessmen and politicians, then as now, have had little patience with the ideal of
learning for its own sake and even less respect for faculty who
often espouse ideas at odds with their views of the purpose and
value of higher education. Today the sums may be larger and
their impact on university research operations greater, but the
pressure to bring universities in line with corporate styles of
accounting and management persists.

The principle of academic freedom articulated a vision of the
university that was at once immune to these powerful interests
and that promised to serve them, however indirectly, by producing new knowledge for the common good. Indeed, academic
freedom rested on the assumption that knowledge and power
were separable; the pursuit of truth ought to have nothing to do
with public conflicts of interest, even if new knowledge could
weigh in on one side or another of one of those conflicts. The
university was defined as "an inviolable refuge from [the] tyranny [of public opinion] . . . an intellectual experiment station,
where new ideas may germinate and where their fruit, though
distasteful to the community as a whole, may be allowed to
ripen."[4] Scientific and social progress depended on the noncon-
formity protected—indeed, fostered—by the university. The
"wellbeing" of the place came from its ability to support critical
thinkers, those who would challenge prevailing orthodoxy and
stir students to think differently, to become "more self-critical,"
hence more likely to bring about change.

The AAUP declaration cited a university president who had
eloquently stated this view: "Certain professors have been refused

reelection lately, apparently because they set their students to thinking in ways objectionable to the trustees. It would be well if more teachers were dismissed because they fail to stimulate thinking of any kind." The professor, the declaration continued, ought to be "a contagious center of intellectual enthusiasm": "It is better for students to think about heresies than not to think at all; better for them to climb new trails and stumble over error if need be, than to ride forever in upholstered ease on the overcrowded highway."[5] The university's function was to offer shelter to these intrepid explorers, to protect them from the cold winds of disapproval that inevitably greeted dissenting ideas.

The faculty considered to be at greatest risk were those in the emerging social science and humanities disciplines.[6] It was precisely because they addressed the question of the moral and social needs of society, because their studies might be disturbing and transformative, that the social sciences most needed the protection of academic freedom. Unlike the mathematical and physical sciences, which, Dewey pointed out, "have secured their independence through a certain abstractness, a certain remoteness from matters of social concern, political economy, sociology, historical interpretation, [and] psychology . . . deal face-to-face with problems of life, not problems of technical theory. Hence the right and duty of academic freedom are even greater here than elsewhere."[7]

Academic freedom, then, formulated as it was in the heyday of Progressivism, aimed to protect those perceived to be most radical, those who were on the front lines of movements of social criticism and social reform. For them, expert knowledge necessarily had an instrumental purpose. The historian-philosopher Michel de Certeau put it this way: "the social sciences born in modern times form a set of institutions that express ethical postulates through technical operations. For a long period, these special institutions organized 'new crusades' of a technical nature to perform ethical tasks."[8] In the early twentieth century, the "crusaders" were (ironically, from today's perspective) overwhelmingly in the field of economics, making readily apparent the tension between critical professorial thinking (knowledge) and business-minded trustees (power). Two examples dramatically illustrate the tension: the experiences of Edward Ross at Stanford and Scott Nearing at the University of Pennsylvania's Wharton School of Business.

Ross was secretary of the American Economic Association when he arrived at Stanford. He believed that "the aim of big business was to throttle social criticism" of the kind he and his fellow Progressives practiced, and his encounters there proved his point.[9] Stanford's founder, Leland Stanford, had been a Republican and a railroad magnate whose business relied on cheap Chinese immigrant labor. Ross quickly (and probably deliberately) incurred the wrath of the founder's widow by supporting socialist Eugene Debs, advocating municipal ownership of utilities, calling for an end to Chinese immigration, and defending the free silver platform of the Democratic party. Mrs. Stanford wrote to the university's president, David Jordan, that Ross's political associations, which "play into the hands of the lowest and vilest elements of socialism," bring "tears to my eyes." Later she insisted that "Professor Ross cannot be trusted, and he should go." Jordan's attempts at negotiation and his appeals to Ross for restraint came to naught and, in 1900, he acquiesced to Mrs. Stanford's wishes by dismissing Ross. In response, seven other faculty members resigned and a group of members of the American Economic Association launched an investigation into the case, "the first professorial inquiry into an academic freedom case," according to historian Walter Metzger, "and a predecessor, if not directly the parent, of the proceedings of Committee A [the Committee on Academic Freedom and Tenure] of the AAUP."[10]

More than a decade later economist Scott Nearing was forced to leave the Wharton School after being attacked by influential alumni. An outspoken socialist whose work addressed the abuses of industrial capitalism, Nearing was let go in 1915 by the president and the board of trustees despite positive recommendations from his department, his chairman, and his dean. He was considered an exceptional teacher, a good administrator, and someone skilled in "the maintenance of student discipline." Although his dean conceded that he had "not been so tactful as he might be," there was no question either about the fulfillment of his duties or of his "moral worthiness."[11] Nor was he said to be lacking in "professorial gumption"—an ambivalent comment, damning in the eyes of a trustee, but praising in the opinion of colleagues and students. Nearing's removal was at least in part the result of three years of campaigning by a group of influential alumni who objected to "the bizarre and radical theories . . . advanced by enthusiastic young instructors . . . [that] are likely to have a poor effect upon Freshmen."[12] These instructors, the alumni went on, "seek publicity by discussion of various public topics in a manner which is likely to arouse class prejudice and fallacious conclusions."[13] Their doctrines, moreover, were "wholly at variance with those of the founder of the Wharton School." The charges became more inflated as they focused on Nearing himself. He was said to have talked "wildly and in a manner wholly inconsistent with Mr. Wharton's well-known views," his "intemperate, persistent and astonishing expressions of untested theories, and . . . [his] unrestrained condemnations of institutions and rules which form the basis of civilized society, passed the most generous bounds of freedom of speech allowed by any institution."[14]

Ross's case precipitated the founding of the AAUP; Nearing's was one of the first cases investigated by the fledgling organization. In neither instance did formal protest by colleagues manage to keep the professor in his job. Both cases starkly posed the problem of knowledge and power: How to protect faculty from the wrath of those upon whom they necessarily depended for financial support?

The AAUP sought to answer that question in at least three ways: by defining the faculty as self-regulating, independent "appointees" (akin to judges in a federal court); by insisting on the knowledge-producing mission of the university itself; and by clarifying the role of its trustees. Since, according to the AAUP's declaration, it is faculty who are trained to produce knowledge—whether as researchers, teachers, or technical experts—it is they who embody the function of the university and so warrant the protection of academic freedom. "A university is a great and indispensable organ of the higher life of a civilized community, in the work of which the trustees hold an essential and highly honorable place, but in which the faculties hold an independent place, with quite equal responsibilities—and in relation to purely scientific and educational questions, the primary responsibility."[15]

If the function of the university is critical thinking, it is the job of trustees to protect it. The AAUP's 1915 declaration compares proprietary institutions (the old model) whose purpose is "not to advance knowledge . . . but rather to subsidize the promotion of the opinions of persons, usually not of the scholar's calling, who provide the funds for their maintenance," with colleges and universities (the modern kind) "not strictly bound . . . to a propagandist duty." These latter are devoted to the public interest, to advancing the common good. They constitute a public trust and so the "trustees are trustees for the public" whether the university is supported by state funds or by private endowment.[16] The trustees' job from this perspective was all-important, according to the "Declaration of Principles," for it involved guaranteeing the upkeep of the university and the autonomy of the faculty. This was a matter not of exercising private proprietorship but of fulfilling a "public trust"; it was a commitment to securing the common good through the advancement of knowledge. "Trustees of . . . universities and colleges have no moral right to bind the reason or the conscience of any professor."[17] Indeed, they must use their power to insulate free inquiry from powerful interests that might corrupt it. Being "trustees for the public" does not mean directly reflecting public opinion since it is likely to be a set of "hasty and unconsidered impulses" based on orthodoxy or ignorance.[18] Rather, it is the protection of the faculty from outside meddling that is the calling of the trustees; only in this way will knowledge be advanced and society improved. Protection meant that trustees must defer to faculty on substantive matters, for they had no competence to judge them. Boards that violate this precept by "exercising an arbitrary power of dismissal" are "barbarous" since they fail to understand the full implications of the distinction between private proprietorship and a public trust.[19] The public trust is that of keeping the "indispensable organ" alive, providing for its physical and financial upkeep while allowing the faculty to breathe freely so that society may progress. This was the "essential nature of a university": it was "a place dedicated to openness of mind."[20] Here the AAUP founders offer a model for university governance that makes protection of academic freedom a moral—indeed, almost a physical—obligation of any board of trustees. "In all . . . domains of knowledge, the first condition of progress is complete and unlimited freedom to pursue inquiry and publish its results. Such freedom is the breath in the nostrils of all scientific activity."[21]

The biological analogy continues with faculty's teaching function—one that reproduces not orthodoxy but the propensity for new thinking in the next generation. Students, the authors insist, must be provided not "ready-made conclusions"; they must be trained "to think for themselves."[22] Even as the anxieties of some of the founding fathers get articulated in the declaration—the need, for example, to treat with great care "immature students," who may be unready to form opinions of their own—the document returns repeatedly to the instructor's "duty" to "give to any students old enough to be in college a genuine intellectual awakening"[23]—an awakening that depends on the student's confidence in the intellectual integrity of the teacher.

> It is clear, however, that this confidence will be impaired if there is suspicion on the part of the student that the teacher is not expressing himself fully or frankly, or that college and university teachers in general are a repressed and intimidated class who dare not speak with that candor and courage which youth always demands in those whom it is to esteem. . . . There must be in the mind of the teacher no mental reservation. He must give the student the best of what he has and what he is.[24]

Of course, the freedom being claimed for faculty entailed "correlative obligations." As researchers, teachers, and expert consultants they must be trained and credentialed according to the rules of their disciplines; without such training their "science" would have no legitimacy. But the articulation and enforcement of professional standards must be left in the hands of the professionals. "It is, in any case, unsuitable to the dignity of a great profession that the initial responsibility for the maintenance of its professional standards should not be in the hands of its own members. It follows that university teachers must be prepared to assume this responsibility for themselves."[25]

The theory of academic freedom goes even further, insisting not only on the moral principle of nonintervention by trustees in faculty work but also on the incompetence of these people to judge the value of the work produced. Academic freedom thus demands extraordinary restraint from those used to exercising power based on judgments they themselves make and outcomes they project and pay for. So it ought not to be surprising that the principle is often ineffective in eliciting that restraint in practice. The long history of AAUP investigations as well as a number of historical studies provide ample documentation of this point.[26] We might say, then, that the theory of academic freedom as it was articulated by Progressives continues to be useful and important because it addresses, although it does not resolve, a tension at the heart of the modern university: that between corporate power and intellectual inquiry, between instrumental knowledge production and open-ended inquiry.

DISCIPLINARY POLITICS

The principle of academic freedom was not, as critics sometimes describe it, an endorsement of the idea that in the university anything goes. The call for faculty autonomy rested on the guarantee of quality provided by disciplinary bodies whose role is to establish and implement norms and standards and so to certify their members' professional competence. Disciplinary associations were depicted as uncorrupted by the play of interests that shaped the world outside the academy, even if the scholars they licensed dealt, as Dewey put it, with "face-to-face problems of life, not with problems of technical theory." Dewey wrote about "an organized society of truth-seekers," by which he meant the newly created disciplinary associations of his day, those intercollegiate bodies that set standards of inquiry and assessed the validity (the apparent scientific quality or truthfulness) of the ideas offered by their members. In return for fulfilling one's responsibilities to the discipline, one received protection from outside intervention.[27]

Disciplinary authorization was meant to defend those whose work was unavoidably controversial against charges of partisanship and from political retribution. If their colleagues attested to the soundness of their methods and the plausibility of their interpretations, these faculty could be represented not as interested parties but as objective seekers after truth.

Yet, as is well known to all of us, disciplinary communities are hierarchical and have a power dynamic of their own. If the community certifies the competence of its members and protects them from external meddling, it also establishes methods of inquiry ("disciplined and systematic training") and standards of judgment ("selecting and recruiting new members") as well as behavioral norms ("cooperating through mutual criticism"). Those who write the history of disciplines and those of us who have broken new ground in our fields know that "discipline" and "disciple" can be synonyms as well as antonyms and that punishment is not always the alternative to discipline but often its regulatory tool. The devastating review, the charges of incomplete research, mockery by one's elders can bring an end to a promising academic career, especially one that engages in a critique of disciplinary premises. These are not external interventions by the incompetent into the workings of the academy; they are internal conflicts, involving not public morality or conventional social belief but disciplinary politics. And, of course, even the line drawn between disciplinary politics and those of the "outside world" is not a clear one since, as Dewey and his colleagues recognized a century ago, research in the human sciences especially is often inspired by contemporary concerns with inevitable political ramifications.

Those of us historians who challenged prevailing views in the name of disciplinary redefinition well remember the kind of opposition we faced when we asked who got to count as a historian, what got to count as history, and how those determinations were made. The critique—and it was a critique in the technical philosophical sense of the term: an interrogation of founding premises, an illumination of methodological and interpretive blind spots—aimed at the very grounds on which the field was based and at the notion that there could be a single prototype of a disciplinary subject. A woman historian was not just a historian with female genitals but someone who might bring different perspectives to her work. How did those perspectives affect the idea of an appropriate historical inquiry? Women's history was not just another topic, a minor theme in the exalted stories of nations and their leaders; it was for many of us an inquiry into the founding assumptions of so-called mainstream history. (African American history, postcolonial history, and queer history offered similar interrogations.)

The reply was often furious, and it wielded the weapons of the strong in a defense of scholarship against corruption by politics. They were professionals—we were politicizing history by exposing the ways in which standards of inclusion effectively discriminated on the basis of gender or race. They were defending the terrain of disinterested history; we were substituting ideology for scholarly rigor. Reviewing a book on nineteenth-century French women, Norman Hampson dismissed it as "uterine history," and Lawrence Stone, offering his ten commandments to historians of women, warned of the dangers of "distorting evidence" to "support modern feminist ideology"—as if the meaning of evidence were unequivocal and otherwise presented no problems about the position, point of view, and interpretations of historians.[28] Accusations from feminists of male bias were greeted as political and ideological; the men's rejection of women's history was taken as a defense of the integrity of the field.

Poststructuralism met an even more vehement refusal, the intensity of which differed according to discipline. Lawrence Stone (erstwhile champion of History) denounced Michel Foucault as a failed or faux historian. Some literary critics (and many others, of course) used Paul de Man's early Nazi writings to call the entire "linguistic turn" into question. The charges of nihilism and moral relativism, of destruction (a play on Jacques Derrida's deconstruction) and irrelevance portrayed the struggle in Manichaean terms. The guardians of orthodoxy were defending mastery and excellence against those who, they claimed, were directly or indirectly bringing political considerations into a hitherto purely objective arena. Hence John Searle: "The biggest single consequence of the rejection of the Western Rationalistic Tradition is that it makes possible an abandonment of traditional standards of objectivity, truth, and rationality, and opens the way for an educational agenda one of whose primary purposes is to achieve social and political transformation."[29]

In 1985, as these struggles were unfolding, a report of AAUP's Committee A warned that orthodoxy might endanger academic freedom, in effect acknowledging the existence of power dynamics internal to disciplinary communities. The report came in response to an inquiry from Stanford law school professor Paul Brest about a comment by Paul Carrington, then dean of the Duke law school. Carrington had written that those who identified with "critical legal studies" disqualified themselves from any law school faculty appointment. The report rejected Carrington's statement, maintaining that belief in the governing principles of a discipline ought not to be a condition of employment:

> In many instances a show of disrespect for a discipline is, at the very same time, an expression of dissent from the prevailing doctrines of that discipline. There is more than a sonant connection between respectfulness and respectability; there is no wide gap between respectability and ideological conventionalism. Thus, while a litmus test of belief in the worth of a subject as a minimum qualification for appointment to a position where one is expected to teach it or teach about it may seem modest in the abstract, on reflection it may prove to be very mistaken; it may end by barring those most like to have remade the field. . . . It is not merely that the long history of academic freedom teaches that charges of irreverence can readily serve as covers to objections to unorthodoxy; rather, it is that it is all but impossible to extenuate the one without abetting the other.[30]

The internal/external, thought/action contrast that makes power and politics the activity of threatening outsiders has, on the one hand, been taken as the necessary condition for faculty and university autonomy, yet—as the AAUP statement makes clear—it also masks the challenge posed by the legitimating disciplinary authority to the free exercise of critical thought. Disciplinary communities provide the consensus necessary to justify academic freedom as a special freedom for faculty. But the inseparable other side of this regulatory and enabling authority is that it can suppress innovative thinking in the name of defending immutable standards. Paradoxically, the very institutions that are meant to legitimize faculty autonomy can also function to undermine it.

ACADEMIC RESPONSIBILITY

There is another area of tension that academic freedom addresses but does not resolve. Like the first two issues I have discussed, it is also the source of controversy and adjudication that never ends. This is the notion of academic responsibility. Conceived as the correlative of academic freedom ("there are no rights without corresponding duties," reads the 1915 "Declaration of Principles"[31]), it was in fact an attempt to bring into being in the very person of the professor the boundary between knowledge and power, thought and action, truth and politics, upon which the principle of academic freedom rested. Academic responsibility referred to the deportment of a faculty member, his performance as an academic subject; it was no longer attached explicitly to the motivation for truth seeking (that was taken to be a freely performed activity, not the fulfillment of a responsibility). Responsibility somehow meant a commitment to keeping thought and politics distinct, or at least to maintaining the appearance of such a distinction, in two ways: in the manner or style of one's academic conduct and in the spatial separation between the world of ideas and the world at large.

The early attempts to separate knowledge and power appealed to the idea of objectivity. The closer scholars could come to it, the more legitimate their work would be, the more the inside could be protected from the outside. The problem, of course, was that—as Dewey and the AAUP founders well knew—work in the human sciences could never claim the objective status of pure science. So, one way of keeping the taint of politics away from scholarship was to displace the problem onto the manner in which ideas were articulated. In the heat of public controversies about the undeniably political ideas of Progressive social scientists, the founders of the AAUP suggested that a faculty member's demeanor could affect the reception of his work. Thus, Dewey noted in 1902 (and the AAUP founders again in 1915) that the deportment of critical scholars could make all the difference. Indeed, they went further, maintaining that academic responsibility demanded that professors set forth their views in "a scholar's spirit," "with dignity, courtesy, and temperateness of language."[32] "It is the manner of conveying the truth," Dewey insisted, that can provoke censure or toleration. (The example he chose is telling for its acknowledgment of the political import of a scholar's ideas and of the challenge they might pose to conventional wisdom.)

> One might, for example, be scientifically convinced of the transitional character of the existing capitalistic control of industrial affairs and its reflected influences upon political life; one might be convinced that many and grave evils and injustices are incident to it, and yet never raise the question of academic freedom. . . . He might go at the problem in such an objective, historic, and constructive manner as not to excite the prejudices or inflame the passions even of those who thoroughly disagreed with him. On the other hand, views at the bottom exactly the same can be stated in such a way as to grasp the feelings of everyone exercising the capitalistic function. What will stand or fall upon its own scientific merits, if presented as a case of objective social evolution, is mixed up with all sorts of extraneous and passion-inflaming factors when set forth as the outcome of the conscious and aggressive selfishness of a class. As a result of such influences the problem of academic freedom becomes to a very large extent a personal matter.[33]

In the classroom, the teacher must be patient, considerate, wise, even as he challenges convention and sparks new thought.

Outside the classroom, he is "under a peculiar obligation to avoid hasty or unverified or exaggerated statements and to refrain from intemperate or sensational modes of expression," even as he exercises "the political rights vouchsafed to every citizen."[34] Recognizing the difficulties of laying down rules for personal conduct ("such rules are likely to be innocuous truisms"), Dewey proceeds, Polonius-like, nonetheless: loyalty to truth, the courage of one's convictions, and respect in the face of controversy are positive traits; conceit, "bumptiousness," "lack of reverence for the things that mean much to humanity," and a "craving for public notoriety" are negative.[35] The aim was not to compromise one's beliefs in order to win public approval but rather to embody something of the "scientific" auspices of ideas in one's very demeanor ("objective, historic, constructive," dispassionate, calm). The notion that personal style might mitigate the impact of one's ideas was, of course, futile.

As the case of Wharton's Scott Nearing suggests, radical substance and radical style were often read as interchangeable, the one implying the other. In the statements I cited from the Wharton School alumni, it is hard to distinguish between "intemperate," "wildly," "astonishing," and "unrestrained," on the one side, and "untested theories" and "fallacious conclusions," on the other. Was Nearing let go because he questioned "the institutions and rules which form the basis of civilized society," or because he lacked the restraint associated with objectivity? Weren't his ideas proof enough that he didn't have the appropriate demeanor? When the trustees came to justify firing Nearing, they were more careful about distinguishing between freedom of expression ("there is not and never will be the slightest wish on the part of the board or of a single of one the trustees to restrict the broadest latitude of opinions, research, and discussion"[36]) and style ("when individual opinions of members of the teaching staff are expressed in a proper manner, upon proper occasions, and with proper respect for the dignity of their relationship to the university . . . such opinions and utterances are welcomed as indicative of progressive growth—no matter how divergent they may be from current or general beliefs"[37]). "Proper" is invoked as something entirely self-evident ("proper manner," "proper occasions," "proper respect"), though, of course, its meaning is completely obscure. Or at least it assumes a shared understanding of what constitutes propriety: commitment to a set of norms that set boundaries both for gentlemanly decorum and gentlemanly ideas, the one being the measure of the other. According to this notion of propriety, it doesn't seem possible that Nearing's manner, however dispassionate, could have offset the objections to his ideas.

Recent controversies about teachers of Middle Eastern studies are only the latest example of the fact that those who disagree with the content of one's teaching often hear it as intemperate, dangerous, and wild, even if the demeanor of the teacher is careful and courteous. It is not easy to separate the contents of the teaching from judgments about the character of the scholar. Still, the emphasis on good manners has never been dropped entirely in AAUP documents and elsewhere in the academy. It stands in the much-cited 1940 statement—in effect a "constitution" for academia. And it has had something of a resurgence these days in administrators' pleas for "civility" and in tests for "collegiality" that, despite AAUP warnings about the discriminatory impact such tests can have, are included in standards for tenure at some universities.[38] The idea that academic deportment ought not to seem political or, better, that the political resonances of academic work can be made acceptable by one's "civility" is still there to be drawn on. As such, it constitutes a check on the notion that academic freedom is about the unqualified autonomy of scholars in their writing and teaching, or at least it poses a serious challenge to that idea.

The second area of academic responsibility is about the spatial separation of activity, captured in the distinction between legitimate scholarly work and "extramural" expression, between acceptable classroom discourse and opinions offered outside that protected space that are not necessarily related to a faculty member's expertise. Was there a responsibility to behave in a certain "academic" manner even when one was exercising one's rights as a citizen? Did the special right of academic freedom entail limits on the public right of free speech? Surely outrageous opinions uttered to the public could redound negatively to the university, imperiling academic freedom within its walls by tarring with the brush of politics the professor's scholarly reputation (and so the university's neutral standing). The 1915 declaration went back and forth. On the one hand, "academic teachers are under a peculiar obligation to avoid hasty or unverified or exaggerated statements, and to refrain from intemperate or sensational modes of expression." On the other hand, they should not have "their freedom of speech, outside the university . . . limited to questions falling within their own specialties." Nor should they be "prohibited from lending their active support to organized movements which they believe to be in the public interest." "It is neither possible nor desirable to deprive a college professor of the political rights vouchsafed to every citizen."[39]

But what of cases of extramural utterance that "raise grave doubts concerning [a faculty member's] fitness for his position?" Should these be treated as a matter of individual conscience or submitted to collective institutional judgment? The question was the subject of much discussion in the drafting of the 1940 statement—a joint endeavor of AAUP (representing faculty) and the Association of American Colleges (representing administrators). The result was a compromise. Paragraph C of the document addressed the issue, but it was followed by an interpretive footnote, so vexed was the problem. The paragraph took the language of the 1915 declaration: the faculty member's "special position in the community imposes special obligations." "He should at all times be accurate, should exercise appropriate restraint, should show respect for the opinions of others, and [this was an addition that imposed a new obligation and suggested that faculty autonomy and university autonomy might be at odds] should make every effort to indicate that he is not an institutional spokesman."[40] The interpretive note actually muddied the issue while exposing the basted seams of compromise. It granted the right of administrators to file charges in an appropriate manner against a faculty member whom they considered to have violated the "admonitions" of paragraph C, but it cautioned that teachers were also citizens and "should be accorded the freedom of citizens."

What this said was that "academic responsibility," as a standard for faculty deportment off campus, could not provide an entirely effective barrier between knowledge and politics. Academic freedom has come to mean the absolute right of a faculty member to "the freedom of citizens" off campus but restrictions on those rights of expression in the classroom. That the matter has not been resolved, however, is indicated by the fact that the vast number of cases investigated by AAUP involve the relationship between a faculty member's extramural speech and his or her fitness as a scholar and teacher. A series of cases illustrates this point.

The first case occasioned a debate among AAUP leaders about the value of invoking "academic responsibility" as a test of professorial merit. It concerned an assistant professor of biology at the University of Illinois in 1963 who wrote a letter to the editor of the student newspaper that so outraged public opinion that he was dismissed by the president. Leo Koch's letter was about sex. In response to an article by two students complaining about the ritualized nature of relations between men and women on campus, Koch counseled greater freedom. Arguing that the students treated the issue too narrowly, he diagnosed a "serious social malaise . . . caused . . . by the hypocritical and downright inhumane moral standards engendered by a Christian code of ethics which was already decrepit in the days of Queen Victoria."[41] The cure was to end the psychological inhibition of healthy needs by condoning sexual intercourse "among those sufficiently mature to engage in it without social consequences [that is, by using modem contraceptives and with good medical advice] and without violating their own codes of morality and ethics."

The response, as one can imagine, was explosive. It was led by the Reverend Ira Latimer, a member of the University of Illinois' Dad's Association, who (following the double standard of the day) wrote to parents of women students. He called Koch's letter "an audacious attempt to subvert the religious and moral foundations of America" and identified it as the "standard operating procedure of the Communist conspiracy."[42] Letters of protest poured in to university administrative offices. Following the recommendations of the executive committee of the College of Liberal Arts and Sciences, the president decided that "Professor Koch's published letter constitutes a breach of academic responsibility so serious as to justify his being relieved of his University duties." He went on: "The views expressed are offensive and repugnant, contrary to commonly accepted standards of morality and their public espousal may be interpreted as encouragement of immoral behavior. It is clear that Mr. Koch's conduct has been prejudicial to the best interests of the university."[43]

Here was a statement that called for condemnation if one took critical thinking to be the mission of the university and if the free speech rights of citizens were to be respected. There was never evidence presented either that Koch (a botanist) uttered these views in his classroom or that he was unfit to teach his subject. Indeed, his colleagues on the faculty senate committee on academic freedom concluded that at most his letter deserved a reprimand. The AAUP investigating committee agreed, concluding that there were administrative violations both procedural and principled, and it called upon the board of trustees to resist public pressure, to "take a broader view of the function of the university and the value of academic freedom . . . to recognize [the university's] maturity, its ability to absorb a few gadflies and its need for uninhibited freedom of discussion."[44]

The investigating committee went on at some length about the utility of the notion of academic responsibility, effectively arguing that in cases of extramural utterance, an individual faculty member's rights as a citizen could not be limited by such a vague and ambiguous term. Citing a passage from John Stuart Mill's *On Liberty*, they maintained that "any serious application of the standard would tend to eliminate or discourage any colorful or forceful utterance. More likely . . . the standard would be reserved as a sanction only for the expression of unorthodox opinion."[45] These comments gave rise to heated debate among the members of Committee A (which receives and acts on these investigatory reports) and to the publication, along with the report, of two statements on academic responsibility, one the majority view, the other, a dissent. While not disagreeing with the investigators' conclusion that Professor Koch had been denied due process and while conceding that "academic responsibility is admittedly very difficult to define," the majority nonetheless insisted that academic responsibility was a standard worth enforcing because "we can hardly expect academic freedom to endure unless it is matched by academic responsibility."[46] The notion might, of course, be abused, but this was not grounds for denying its importance. "The remedy is, instead, insistence on proper procedural safeguards, a highly significant role for the faculty . . . and a vigilant oversight by this Association."[47]

The dissenters were not convinced. They insisted that the majority had misinterpreted the 1940 statement, which, on the question of speech outside the classroom, was unambiguous: "by law, in the expression of his opinions, the teacher is no less free than other citizens."[48] The only legitimate ground for dismissal was—historically and in the present—"demonstrated unfitness to teach." "To speak of 'academic responsibility' as a standard or test for dismissal because a teacher has expressed an unpopular opinion without anchoring it to unmistakable particulars is to waver on a floating bog of semantics."[49]

A special standard of academic responsibility, the dissenters continued, not only treated teachers differently from other citizens but it opened "a Pandora's box of all the coercive and compulsive crusades of sectarian, political, and economic pressure groups together with consequent attempts at dismissal by administrators who are unable to resist the public pressure engendered by such groups whose causes often contain more heat than light."[50]

Oberlin College English professor Warren Taylor, the author of the dissent, undoubtedly had the previous decade's experience in mind. During the McCarthy period, many faculty were fired, some for having admitted to membership in the Communist Party, some for simply having been accused of such membership, some for having declined to name names, and others for having taken the Fifth Amendment. "Academic responsibility" was directly or indirectly used as a justification for these firings.

Sometimes the need to protect the university from legislative intervention was the reason, sometimes the refusal of the professor to come clean with his colleagues inside the university was the issue, sometimes it was that communism was by definition antithetical to free thought. Thus, the American Committee for Cultural Freedom (the group of Cold War intellectuals founded in 1951) argued that "a member of the Communist Party has transgressed the canons of academic responsibility, has engaged his intellect to servility, and is therefore professionally disqualified from performing his functions as a teacher."[51] This logic substituted for any need to provide concrete evidence of scholarly or pedagogic unfitness. And it ruled out the possibility that, for some faculty at least, communism was more about developing a critical theory of society than it was about offering unquestioned obeisance to the Soviet state.

Most often, as Warren Taylor had predicted, academic responsibility was invoked when administrators or trustees were unable to resist public pressure to punish a professor whose off-campus speech had offended their sensibilities. In these cases, the responsibility was not to think freely (not to exemplify the function of the university) but to protect the public reputation of the university (by refraining from the expression of critical ideas). AAUP investigators found themselves time and again arguing against administrative judgments "in applying what are necessarily somewhat imprecise standards for the limits of propriety of extramural controversy."[52] In most of these instances, in fact, faculty committees (and AAUP investigators) made a case for a professor whose extramural speech was deemed outrageous based not on the content or style of that speech but on the fairness (according to AAUP recommendations) of procedures followed in judging the individual and, usually more importantly, on the quality of his or her professional standing as a scholar and teacher.

In this they carefully restricted "academic responsibility" to the fulfillment of teaching and disciplinary requirements, thereby reinforcing the distinction between knowledge production and politics as forms of activity, not as personal qualities that separated professors from ordinary people. That they did not usually prevail is an indication, I think, of the difficulty of maintaining the distinction in practice.

The case of Angela Davis provides another illustration of the way in which "academic responsibility" could be used. When Davis was not renewed as a lecturer in philosophy at UCLA in 1970 because of her membership in the Communist Party and because in public speeches she attacked police as "pigs" and maintained that academic freedom was an "'empty concept' if divorced from freedom of political action or if 'exploited' to maintain such views as the genetic inferiority of black people,"[53] her colleagues argued that nothing in her lectures or classroom behavior indicated dereliction of duty. Students talked about her courses as rigorous and open-minded; they were not expected to parrot her conclusions, which were, in any case, offered as tentative interpretations. If her off-campus rhetoric was inflated, inaccurate, and even "distasteful and reprehensible," it had not spilled over into her research and teaching. One of the few regents who opposed her firing noted that "in this day and age when the decibel level of political debate . . . has reached the heights it has, it is unrealistic and disingenuous to demand as a condition of employment that the professor address political rallies in the muted cadences of scholarly exchanges. Professors are products of their times even as the rest of us."[54]

Absent here was the idea that "academic responsibility" extended beyond one's purely academic responsibilities. Although the style and manner of one's performance still counted (Davis was said to be as calm in the classroom as she was outrageous in public), it did so only within the walls of academe. Although this was the dissenting opinion of a regent in the Davis case, it came increasingly to characterize the restriction of the notion of academic responsibility to things academic. There was indeed a separation between knowledge and politics, but an academic could participate in both as long as she distinguished between her roles as a scholar and a citizen. Academic freedom was meant to guarantee this separation in theory, difficult as it might be to maintain in practice.

But what if a professor's political engagement led to revelations about the quality of his scholarship? This is what happened in the case of Ward Churchill at the University of Colorado. Churchill's reference to the World Trade Tower September 11, 2001, victims as "little Eichmanns" who deserved their fate, infuriated the regents of the university. In response to demands from the regents and the governor that he be fired immediately, the administration of the university (following AAUP procedures) asked a faculty committee to examine his professional competence. The inquiry into his work produced information about "research misconduct" considered so damning that neither the committee nor the AAUP felt they could come to his rescue. It was certainly true, his colleagues conceded, that there would have been no examination of his scholarly opus if the political charges hadn't been made; yet, given the questionable nature of his academic credentials and the extensive criticism that came from within his own field of American Indian studies, it was extremely difficult to make a strong bid for his retention.

Although the Churchill and Davis cases differed on the question of the scholarly integrity and teaching performance of the professor, both were fired and for the same reasons: their extramural speech incurred the wrath of outside groups whose power influenced the decisions of university administrators. These were

cases that revealed the weakness of the notion that a full separation was in fact possible between thought and action, scholarship and politics. Academic freedom was easily compromised by
a notion of academic responsibility that could be extended to
include the responsibility to protect the university from exactly
those forces that Dewey and his colleagues in 1915, and Warren
Taylor and his fellow dissenters in 1963, warned would compromise its mission of free and critical inquiry.

BLURRED BOUNDARIES

In 1970, in the context of the heated politics of the Vietnam
War, the AAUP issued a statement on "academic responsibility" that, while recognizing how politics had become part of
campus life, insisted on what had by then become the classic
distinction between the scholar and the citizen. "Because academic freedom has traditionally included the instructor's full
freedom as a citizen, most faculty members face no insoluble
conflicts between the claims of politics, social action, and conscience, on the one hand, and the claims and expectations of
their students, colleagues, and institutions on the other."[55]

As the subsequent years of political and epistemological
turmoil (identity politics, culture wars, and science wars; linguistic and cultural turns; structuralism and poststructuralism) would reveal, however, what is missing in those sharp
distinctions between outside/inside, power/knowledge, action/
thought, politics/truth is, ironically, the idea that one's sense
of responsibility as a citizen could legitimately affect one's
scholarship—ironically because among the members of AAUP
were many who, like the founding Progressive fathers, were
motivated by concerns about the direction of society, the

organization of the economy, and the conduct of politics to undertake the research and teaching that earned them scholarly distinction. As in the attempt to mask with good manners the political implications of academic research, so the consignment of politics to "extramural" speech, while it offered an important way of defending a professor's rights as a citizen, left aside the more difficult question of how and whether contemporary concerns (the stuff of political contests) might legitimately and explicitly be addressed by scholars in their capacity as teachers and researchers.

Where is the line between polemical advocacy and critical scholarship in work that rereads the history of democracy as a story of the exclusion of differences based on ethnicity, gender, and race? It may be relatively simple to decide that a teacher of women's studies who requires that students share her outrage at all things "patriarchal" is unwisely polemical in her pedagogy, or that a chemistry professor's use of class time to denounce the war in Iraq is inappropriate, but the tougher questions involve scholarly interpretations—what might be called the point of view that necessarily informs research, writing, and teaching in the humanities and social sciences. In a 2008 book, the literary scholar and academic administrator Stanley Fish has cautioned academics to "save the world on your own time," urging us to teach the facts or the texts in our chosen fields without taking a position on them.[56] Fish adheres to the idea that politics and scholarship are entirely separable entities. But the separation between them is easier in theory than in practice since taking positions—on the quality of evidence used to support interpretations, on the reliability of certain methods of investigation, on the premises of the writers of texts and textbooks, on the ethical issues—is part of the scholar's job, part of what makes her a compelling and inspiring teacher. Moreover, those positions are not neutrally arrived at by, say, balancing all sides until an objective view emerges; rather, they are the result of some kind of deeply held political or ethical commitment on the part of the professor. The tension between professorial commitments and academic responsibility is an ongoing one that the principle of academic freedom is meant to adjudicate.

In recent years, the blurring of the lines between politics and scholarship, the acknowledgment that there is some connection, has opened the way for full-fledged political assaults on university teachers: from the Israel lobby's attacks on Middle Eastern studies courses that address the ethics of the occupation and the rights of Palestinians or that simply employ professors whose loyalty to current Israeli policy is in question; from evangelical Christians who oppose the teaching of evolution in the biology curriculum or classes that question their views of sexual morality; from organized student groups—right and left—who find themselves made "uncomfortable" by readings assigned in courses; from right-wing trustees and alumni who feel that "public tax dollars should not be used to promote political, religious, ideological or cultural beliefs or values as truth when such values are in conflict with the values of American citizenship and the teaching of Western Civilization."[57] Despite the valiant efforts of some administrators to resist the pressure, these groups have had an impact (a chilling effect) on the organization of the curriculum, on the hiring and firing of faculty, and on the kinds of speakers and conferences permitted on campuses.

When administrators do resist the pressure, it is in the name of academic freedom, the right—indeed, the necessity of autonomy for a self-regulating faculty, and this is a demonstration of the continuing value of the concept, whatever its inherent tensions and limitations. In pointing out the ongoing tensions that the principle of academic freedom mediates, I do not mean to call its utility into question. On the contrary, it seems to me that it is precisely because the tensions evident a century ago continue to trouble the relationships among faculty, administrators, and boards of trustees; because the value of critical thinking is regularly under siege in the disciplines, the universities, and the nation; and because the tensions I have been describing are not susceptible to final resolution that we need this principle in our ongoing struggle to preserve that which is best about universities and university education—the commitment to free and unfettered inquiry as an ideal we reach for, even as its attainment never seems quite complete.

3

CIVILITY, AFFECT, AND ACADEMIC FREEDOM

In August 2014 Steven Salaita was scheduled to take up a position as a tenured associate professor in the American Indian and Indigenous Studies program at the University of Illinois at Urbana-Champaign. Salaita had resigned his job at Virginia Tech, where he had tenure, and ordered books and submitted syllabuses for his new courses at UIUC. He had every reason to believe his future was secure. Although his appointment was contingent on a final approval by the board of trustees, which would meet two weeks after the school year began, Salaita had been assured that this was merely a formality. It wasn't: The board refused to ratify his appointment.[1]

The reason was the uproar over his comments on Twitter, where Salaita had condemned—often using fierce invective— Israel's violence during its 2014 military attack on Gaza. Well-organized supporters of Israel alerted the university to his tweets, accused him of anti-Semitism, and questioned his scholarship as well as his political judgment. Salaita's scholarship, on colonial settler occupations, has been critical of Israeli policy toward the Palestinians. Protesters deluged the chancellor's office with emails warning that if Salaita were hired, they would withdraw their support of the university. After meeting with the university president and the board of trustees in late July, the chancellor, Phyllis Wise, informed Salaita that she could not recommend him to the board. Wise stated that the impassioned rhetoric of his tweets was a sure sign of his behavior as a teacher; he would be intolerant in the classroom, threatening the comfort, safety, and security of his students. There was no evidence for this inference from tweets to classroom: Salaita's record at Virginia Tech indicated he was a respected teacher, tolerant of a wide range of ideas. But for Wise, that evidence was beside the point. In her letter, the chancellor drew attention to civility, emphasizing it as a requirement for the exercise of academic freedom: "What we cannot and will not tolerate at the University of Illinois are personal and disrespectful words or actions that demean and abuse either viewpoints themselves or those who express them."[2]

In the wake of the Salaita case, AAUP vice president Hank Reichman posted a blog under the heading "Is 'Incivility' the New Communism?"[3] He cited a number of instances in which criticism of Israel in the name of justice for Palestinians had led university administrators to impose disciplinary penalties on the critics. Salaita was fired—or not appointed (depending on your interpretation of contract law)—because the chancellor insisted that his tweets during the Gaza War lacked civility; a student at Ohio University was reprimanded by the university president for lacking civility in her failure to consider the feelings of other members of the university "family" when she staged a dramatic protest against Israel's abuse of Palestinians; and Nicholas Dirks, chancellor at UC Berkeley, set the terms by which future punishment might be imposed: "We can only exercise our right to free speech insofar as we feel safe and respected in doing so, and this in turn requires that people treat each other with civility. Simply put, courteousness and respect in words and deeds are basic preconditions to any meaningful exchange of ideas. In this sense, free speech and civility are two sides of a single coin—the coin of open, democratic society."[4]

A few days later, Reichman posted another blog, this one titled "And Now There's a Blacklist?"[5] There he continued the comparison to the 1950s "Red Scare," citing the AMCHA Initiative's public list of 218 faculty members in Middle East studies programs who had signed the petition for boycott, divestment, and sanctions against the Israeli occupation. AMCHA, which means "your people" in Hebrew, was founded in 2011 in California; its motto is "protecting Jewish students." Urging wide dissemination of the names on its list, AMCHA charged the professors not just with anti-Semitism but with violations of American law. "Many of these patently biased boycotters of Israel are affiliated with government-designated, taxpayer-funded National Resource Centers (NRC) on their campuses," they wrote. By "publicly vilifying Israel," the complaint went on, these supporters "violated both the letter and spirit of the federal law which funds their teaching and research."[6] Here AMCHA was referring to the State Department's fact sheet on anti-Semitism, which goes beyond the European Monitoring Center on Racism and Xenophobia's references to Jews by including a whole section on "anti-Semitism relative to Israel."[7] The AMCHA list, then, not only warned Jewish students to avoid taking courses with (to boycott?) these dangerous teachers, it also identified these teachers as subversives to their employers and to the public at large.

AMCHA is not alone but is only the most recent effort to rid universities of faculty critical of Israel's treatment of Palestinians. There is the ongoing work (since 1987) of Abraham Foxman and the Anti-Defamation League; there are also Daniel Pipes's Campus Watch founded in 2002, Scholars for Peace in the Middle East, a pro-Israel group created in the same year, and David Horowitz's online magazine *Frontpage*, to name just a few. The McCarthy-like campaign has been going on for a long time. If anti-Americanism was the slogan of Red Scare patriots, anti-Semitism is the smear attached to critics of the Israeli occupation. And although there is no senator from Wisconsin waving lists of subversives, these organizations and the individuals associated with them have had a powerful effect on freedom of speech at colleges and universities in this country. There are very visible contests—the attacks on Columbia University professor Rashid Khalidi when he was nominated for the Edward Said chair at Princeton in 2005 and other denunciations of his pro-Palestinian positions that led to his removal that year from a New York City teacher-training program; the denial of tenure in 2007 to Norman Finkelstein at DePaul and to Mehrene Larudee, the colleague who supported him and shared his views on Palestine; the David Project at Columbia, which sought (unsuccessfully) to have Joseph Massad fired but which wreaked havoc with the Middle Eastern Studies program there; a similar (also unsuccessful) vitriolic campaign to prevent the tenuring of Nadia Abu el-Haj at Barnard—both in 2007; the Steven Salaita case in 2014. In addition there are many more instances of nonrenewals of contracts, refusals of employment, and forced resignations of scholars and others (usually with no due process whatsoever) for the slightest evidence of skepticism about Israel's treatment of Palestinians. Arun Gandhi's blog in the *Washington Post* in 2008 calling for peace and nonviolence to ensure the future of Israel (entitled "Jewish Identity Can't Depend on Violence") caused such an outcry (Foxman labeled it "shameful" and anti-Semitic) that the president of the University of Rochester demanded his resignation as director of the M. K. Gandhi Institute for Nonviolence, even after he apologized for his "poorly worded comments."[8] In 2014 the Reverend Bruce M. Shipman, the chaplain at Yale's Episcopal Church, resigned under pressure because of a letter he had written to the *New York Times* in which he had suggested that concern about anti-Semitism in Europe "makes far too little of the relationship between Israel's policies in the West Bank and Gaza." According to newspaper reports, "Critics said that he was blaming Jews for anti-Semitism, a charge he denied. Shipman told the [New Haven] *Register* that he resigned because he did not have enough support from his board. He said he had received 'an avalanche of hate mail' since his letter was published."[9] (Hate mail, by the way, is a favorite weapon of the crusaders against the critics of Israel.)

Although not all of the objections to the critics of Israel explicitly raise the specter of incivility, I think Reichman is right to caution us about the increasing use of that term not only to deride unruly behavior but to deem certain scholars, their scholarship, and their opinions unacceptable. If criticism of Israel is necessarily anti-Semitic, that logic goes, it is by definition uncivil (its expression is hurtful to Jews), hence it is outside the pale of tolerable ideas and so legitimately censored. As in Dirks's pronouncement, there is no academic freedom possible for ideas and actions that don't meet the civility test—"free speech and civility," he said, "are two sides of a single coin."[10]

The many objections to Dirks rejected the idea that civility had anything to do with free speech; they reminded him that the public sphere (of which the university is a part) is a noisy, contentious, emotionally fraught space. Michael Meranze pointed out that "ultimately the call for civility is a demand that you not express anger; and if it was enforced it would suggest that there is nothing to be angry about in the world."[11] The leaders of the American Historical Association wrote that the democratic public sphere must rest "on the recognition that speech on matters of public concern is often emotional and that it employs a variety of idioms and styles. Hence American law protects not only polite discourse but also vulgarity, not only sweet rationality, but also impassioned denunciation."[12]

From one perspective, Reichman is right—incivility is in our era what communism was in the 1950s and 1960s. In both instances the denial of academic freedom to individuals and groups is based on the idea that their views place them outside the community of rational discourse. Just as communists were denied constitutional rights because they were said not to believe in them, proponents of Palestinian rights are tarred with the brushes of terrorism and anti-Semitism and silenced. There are nonetheless important differences between them that have everything to do with the different moments in which the terms became rallying cries for repression. To be un-American in the 1950s and 1960s meant to hold *ideas* taken to be antithetical to the political order, to endorse a social and economic system that would change relations of power in the country. A communist was a political enemy of the state. In contrast, incivility has a seemingly apolitical aspect; it refers to the disgusting or intemperate or disrespectful behavior of individuals as it impacts other individuals. It is about *affect*, not ideas.

INCIVILITY'S HISTORY

Of course, the charge of incivility can be a mask for a certain politics—as the Israel/Palestine examples clearly indicate. The long history of the notion of civility shows that it has everything to do with class, race, and power. But it is not about the ideas one espouses; it has to do instead with one's public performance and its assessment by others—a performance, moreover, that requires the suppression of one's true beliefs, feelings, and desires. The French writer Mirabeau noted in the 1760s that civility only presents "the mask of virtue and not its face."[13] Norbert Elias cited Erasmus's "On Civility in Boys" (1530) as an early example of a guide to manners for the upwardly mobile. If "a peasant wipes his nose on his cap and coat, a sausage maker on his arm and elbow," the boy is warned that his hand is no more acceptable. "It is more decent to take up the snot in a cloth, preferably while turning away."[14] Elias was especially interested in the sociopsychic consequences of the civilizing process, in pressures on the lower orders to assimilate to the manners of their superiors by repressing their "affective impulses." It is fear, he says, that motivates adherence to codes of conduct; parents instill it in their children "as much by gestures as by words." He goes on to show how the concept of civility was tied to definitions of civilization as Western states consolidated and expanded their colonial reach, defining as their mission the diffusion of their standards to "simpler and more primitive people."[15] Primitives were routinely referred to as barbarians and savages, terms applied to the domestic lower classes as well as to colonial subjects. Elias writes that the strict code of manners for the upper class was "an instrument of prestige, but . . . also . . . an instrument of power. It is not a little characteristic of the structure of Western society that the watchword of its colonizing movement is 'civilization.'"[16]

Scholars have documented these power differentials and how notions of civility were used to define them. Kathleen Brown describes the association of civility with cleanliness in sixteenth-century America: "Writers documenting contact with Native Americans and West Africans evoked civility in exclusive ways, conjuring fears of animal natures unmitigated by Christian virtue and foreshadowing the meanings attached to civilization a century later."[17] William Chafe points out that during the sit-ins in Greensboro, North Carolina, peaceful demonstrators—deliberately conducting themselves respectably and in a nonviolent manner as they claimed their civil rights—were charged with incivility.[18] John Murray Cuddihy, a sociologist of religion, wrote of the effects of what he called "the Protestant etiquette" on "emancipated" Jewish intellectuals. The problem for these men (Karl Marx, Sigmund Freud, and Claude Lévi-Strauss) was at once to live by the codes of decorum their societies required for success and to wrestle with the designation of their kind as the embodiment of incivility: obsessive, fanatical, vulgar, effeminate, unrestrained—the disruptive Jewish id to the responsible Christian superego.[19]

The Ordeal of Civility, the apposite title of Cuddihy's book, is a good alternative description of the bourgeois public sphere famously characterized by Jürgen Habermas as democratic, open, and accessible—the realm of rational discourse in which, it was claimed, anyone could participate. As the political theorist Nancy Fraser has argued, the dissident claims of minority groups go unheard in the public sphere when they are tagged as departures from the protocols of style and decorum—dismissed as evidence of irrationality and so placed outside the realm of what is taken to be reasoned deliberation.[20] They are by definition uncivil, and thus beneath contempt. Once a certain space or style of argument is identified as civil, the implication is that dissenters from it are uncivilized. "Civility" becomes a synonym for orthodoxy; "incivility" designates unorthodox ideas or behavior.

That is how I understand the results of a survey of college and university administrators reported by *Inside Higher Ed* in 2104 that found that "a majority of provosts are concerned about declining faculty civility in American higher education."[21] And that is how I interpret a friend's (puzzled) report that the president of his university privately reprimanded him for his "uncivil remarks" after a faculty meeting at which he had expressed concern (in polite and muted tones) about how the university handled financial aid for African American students on his campus.

More recently, the affective dimension of incivility has been further narrowed to refer to a failure to take into account the feelings of those who may be hurt or made uncomfortable by one's remarks, comments, ideas, or political opinions. The University of Missouri's "Show Me Respect" project includes a "toolbox" that offers twenty ways to achieve civility (including the reminder to "do unto others as you would have them do unto you").[22] At the University of Wisconsin, Oshkosh, a 2011 conference offered these words of wisdom: "Academic freedom and free speech require open, safe, civil and collegial campus environments."[23] And a statement from a University of Maryland discussion paper on civility in 2013 defines it "simply as 'niceness to others.' . . . Additionally, the definition may be used broadly to spur discussions on how 'nice guys and gals finish first' and how cordiality and kindness can be tracked across campus to ensure faculty, staff, and students are indeed playing nice."[24]

The purported or potential hurtfulness of expression has now become the grounds for censoring it. So it was that Dirks framed his association of free speech and civility: "We can only exercise our right to free speech insofar as we *feel safe* and respected in doing so, and this in turn requires that people treat each other with civility."[25] When civility is synonymous with safety, verbal utterance is equated not only with psychic but with physical harm. It is in these terms that the Zionist organization AMCHA defines its mission to "protect Jewish students from both direct and indirect assault and fear while attending colleges and universities."[26] Here the group takes strategic advantage of the prevailing discourse on civility, conjuring up the threat of terrorist attacks ("fear," "direct assault") to advance a very specific political agenda. One of AMCHA's founders, Tammi Benjamin, claims that anti-Semitism in the University of California system is seeded by "foreign students" who come from "relentlessly anti-Semitic Arab cultures" and "have ties to terrorist organizations."[27]

But the charge of physical or emotional assault as a mask for political or intellectual disagreement is limited neither to supporters of Israel nor to academic administrators. The affective test for censoring speech is being used by some representatives of women, minorities (racial, ethnic, sexual), and others intent on addressing inequities of treatment and discrimination on campuses. They are joined by moralists of all stripes, among them those whose religious conscience or social sensibilities are offended by profanity and references to abortion or homosexuality and those who seek at all costs to avoid the repetition of perceived trauma.[28] What is disturbing is the convergence of right and left around claims of personal injury, presented less as an experience of inequality (although that is not entirely absent) than as a question of what Wendy Brown calls the depreciation of individual human capital. In her brilliant analysis of the rationality of neoliberalism, Brown talks about the way "homo oeconomicus" has come to stand for everything human, eclipsing "homo politicus" and all other aspects of being human. Neoliberal rationality, she argues, is "ubiquitous today in statecraft and the workplace, in jurisprudence, education, culture, and a vast range of quotidian activity. . . ." She defines it as "a peculiar form of reason that configures all aspects of existence in economic terms," and "is quietly undoing basic elements of democracy."[29] I want to argue that the insistence on individual injury, on the need to secure the safety, security, and comfort of students on campus, resonates with the program of neoliberal rationality. What I've been calling the affective turn, even in antidiscrimination discourse, is ultimately about the entitlements of individual students to comfort, safety, and conscience; to the right to maximize one's value; and to do so free of distractions and impediments.[30]

The willingness of universities to capitulate to these student demands is another aspect of neoliberal rationality: the redefinition of the mission of the university as a service delivered to paying clients. Chris Lorenz describes it this way: "Because this view represents education as a free and equal exchange between equally positioned buyers and sellers, the hierarchical relationship between teachers and those being taught disappears, and this suggests that the purchasers of education have a right to get what they paid for. To make matters worse, because the customer is always right in the market, students in the education market are also always right."[31] In other words, student feelings are now placed on an equal—if not superior—plane with a professor's pedagogical judgment and his or her disciplinary expertise. Perhaps the most glaring example of this is the recurrence of cases in which administrators insist that professors raise the grades of students who complain that they have been shortchanged for the quantity of work they have done in a course. (The question of quality is no longer a valid consideration.[32]) But it is not exactly equality that is invoked in the reconfigured student–teacher relationship; or perhaps it is better to call it a peculiar kind of equality in which the commanding position of students rests on their being portrayed as vulnerable victims who need the protection of adults—of professors, university administrators, and government officials. Whether positioned as client or consumer or victim, the student is allowed to call the shots.

In the new corporate model, universities have turned to such nonacademic organizations as the National Center for Higher Education Risk Management, a law and consulting practice that, since 2000, has offered advice about matters ranging from problem drinking to sexual harassment, student suicide, threat assessment, and much more.[33] The notion that universities are in the business of risk management signifies, Lorenz says, the primacy of financial over educational considerations in academic institutions. This in turn has enhanced the claim to more power for trustees, whose preeminent authority was once modified by a conception of governance shared with administrators and faculty. In 2014 the Project on Governance for a New Era, supported by the American Council of Trustees and Alumni and written by Benno Schmidt, produced a report that called upon trustees to "take a more active role in reviewing and benchmarking the work of faculty and administrators and monitoring outcomes. . . . They must not be intermittent or passive fiduciaries of a billion dollar industry critical to the preparation of America's next leaders."[34]

The result of these processes of individualization and corporatization is not only to rule out faculty autonomy in their areas of disciplinary and educational expertise but also (as Brown points out) to subvert claims for racial, gender, and sexual equality by redefining them in terms of rights to individual security and comfort, or to abandon them altogether. And it transforms the university from a place where ideas are contested, debated, and exchanged to one in which vigilant risk managers allow consumers to influence what can and cannot be said—controlled economies replace the liberal marketplace of ideas. In this way the justification for academic freedom, an element of democracy as Brown defines it, comes undone.

HATE SPEECH AND
AFFIRMATIVE ACTION

The emergence of the affective turn dates back to 1980s controversies over hate speech codes on campuses. This was a moment when the increased presence of women and minorities at colleges and universities drew attention to persistent patterns of discrimination and to demands that they be addressed. There was now a critical mass of previously excluded newcomers that enabled new forms of campus collective action. The question of affirmative action in employment and education was being hotly disputed, and the courts weighed in with a variety of decisions, many of which emphasized the need to demonstrate individual injury in discrimination and class action suits and so moved the focus from groups to individuals. The courts also dealt differentially with First Amendment cases, tending to favor appeals from libertarian and right-wing groups to guarantee individual rights of free speech over those from the left, which emphasized social justice and political dissidence. This was the framework within which speech codes proliferated. The justification for them came from critical race theorists, among others, who argued that "fighting words" and group defamation didn't deserve First Amendment protection. Speech was action, they insisted. They used the language of psychological injury (in effect prescribed by the courts) to make their case, pointing out (not incorrectly) that hate speech was hurtful, that those minorities it targeted were usually not in a position to fight back, and that, in terms of impact, there was no effective difference between verbal and physical assault. The resultant lack of self-esteem suffered by individuals was said to satisfy the legal test for discriminatory harassment: conduct "so severe and objectively offensive that it effectively bars the victim's access to an educational opportunity or benefit."[35]

The carefully crafted arguments of critical legal theorists were meant to expose larger discriminatory patterns (the psychic harms that minorities suffered were offered as the concrete embodiments of structures of racism and sexism), but they also opened a Pandora's box that resulted in the dilution (or cooptation?) of their aims. The University of Connecticut's speech code (eventually abandoned under threat of litigation) is a good example of the blunting of the critical edge of these arguments. The rules were meant to secure for individuals and groups "a positive environment in which everyone feels comfortable working or living."[36] A broader example was the creation on many campuses of "diversity workshops" run by newly minted experts, who sought to rein in racist and sexist epithets by having students who were the targets of them tell the perpetrators how bad it made them feel—empathy, it was believed, would cure the problem of discrimination.[37]

This kind of wishful thinking, critics warned, did not address structures of inequality, making them instead a matter of an individual's ill intention, on the one side, and another individual's injury, on the other. While civil liberties groups worried (rightly) that regulating speech in this way posed a threat to individual rights protected by the First Amendment, others pointed to the depoliticizing effect the codes had. Judith Butler, for example, objected to the conflation of speech and conduct on both philosophical and political grounds. Not only does the claim that speech is action overstate the power of language, she argued, it attributes causality to an individual speaker's words that ignores the function of racist language as a continuation of racist social practices and institutions. Language doesn't originate with the speaker, it refers to already understood beliefs that inhere in a community of shared ideas and institutional conditions. Punishing or censoring individual speech distracts from the need to alter and confront these conditions:

> When the scene of racism is reduced to a single speaker and his or her audience, the political problem is cast as the tracing of the harm as it travels from the speaker to the psychic/somatic constitution of the one who hears the term or to whom it is directed. The elaborate institutional structures of racism as well as sexism are suddenly reduced to the scene of utterance, and utterance, no longer the sedimentation of prior institution and use, is invested with the power to establish and maintain the subordination of the group addressed.[38]

Moreover, Butler continued, the assumption that language produces a predictable, singular effect denies agency to those (individuals and groups) targeted by it and conceives of them as impotent victims; they have no other recourse than to call on the power of university administrators or government officials to protect them. Henry Louis Gates characterized this as "the seductive vision of the therapeutic state,"[39] and wondered how and why things had so dramatically changed since the 1960s, when the aim was not "to enlist power" but to resist it.[40]

THE COMFORT OF STUDENTS

If anything, the attention to individual injury seems to have intensified in the last few years. Although the call for "civility" suggests concern about the public sphere, in fact it is individual discomfort that is at issue in case after case. So, to return to the Salaita firing, the chancellor's ostensible concern for the comfort of some Jewish students (and many more donors) justified her breaking all the rules of faculty governance and administrative procedure. Although there was clear evidence of what can only be called politics, she emphatically (and disingenuously) denied it, insisting that her only aim was to protect students from the discomfort of Salaita's controversial views.[41]

There may be a political dimension to the new attention to microaggressions—the often inadvertent but potentially hurtful remarks that may refer to members of minority groups—but it is hard to see it that way. The author of an influential book on the topic, Derald Wing Sue, a professor of psychology and education at Teachers College, Columbia University, emphasizes the need for colleges to "maintain safe environments for their increasingly diverse work forces and student bodies."[42] To do this, he suggests, requires attention to the harm that even seemingly innocent words can inflict, harm measured by a student's testimony to his or her discomfort. Of course, the line between subtle racism, sexism, or homophobia and political opinion can be hazy, as is the question of what counts as insult in a classroom setting or, for that matter, in any student–teacher or student–student relationship. I have no objection to students condemning outright racist or sexist remarks directed jokingly or seriously at them. The right to free speech is not a right to irresponsible pedagogy; that pedagogy should be challenged and dealt with. But the movement to expose microaggressions usually refers less to instances of that kind than to inadvertent comments or to opinions deemed politically incorrect. Does criticism of affirmative action, for example, count as microaggression? Is the individual's perception the only measure of the harm said to have been done? How has the attention to microaggressions distracted from what might be called macroaggressions—that is, to identifiably objectionable comments? And how has an increasingly exclusive preoccupation with the nuances of hateful speech taken attention away from the policies and institutions that enable it: things like the way financial aid is distributed, living space organized, fraternities regulated (or not), and admissions policies implemented? Butler puts it sharply:

> That words wound seems incontestably true, and that hateful, racist, misogynist homophobic speech should be vehemently countered seems incontrovertibly right. But does understanding from where speech derives its power to wound alter our conception of what it might mean to counter that wounding power? Do we accept the notion that injurious speech is attributable to a singular subject and act? If we accept such a juridical constraint on thought . . . as a point of departure, what is lost from the political analysis of injury? Indeed, when political discourse is fully collapsed into juridical discourse, the meaning of political opposition runs the risk of being reduced to the act of prosecution.[43]

Butler wrote those words in the context of the 1980s and 1990s debates about campus speech codes; they are still applicable today when, once again (or still), arguments about the psychic impact of structures of discrimination have been coopted by neoliberal individualist discourses. When detecting microaggressions changes the conversation from structures of inequality to personal injuries, political discourse (and the action it conceives) can become disturbingly silent.

Then there is the movement for trigger warnings, which began with feminist objections to graphic discussions of rape online and has now morphed into a nightmare of calls for the suppression of speech. Trigger warnings are meant to prevent emotional stress for students who have experienced some kind of trauma—the definition has gotten wider and wider—by alerting them to potentially uncomfortable items on a course syllabus and even excusing them from the assignment. The AAUP report on the topic cited Oberlin College's original policy (which was tabled to allow more faculty discussion) as an example of the extremes to which concern about triggers might lead. The college's policy listed possible trigger topics as including "racism, classism, sexism, heterosexism, cissexism, ableism and other issues of privilege and oppression." Chinua Achebe's novel *Things Fall Apart* might "trigger readers who have experienced racism, colonialism, religious persecution, violence, suicide and more."[44] A friend told me that he was cautioned not to use the word "suicide" in a presentation he gave at Amherst College. On a *New Yorker* blog, Harvard Law School professor Jeannie Suk Gerson worried that hard-fought feminist reforms about rape law were being undermined by her students' reluctance to talk about rape and to debate what counts and doesn't count as consent, coercion, and crime—topics necessary for the teaching of the subject. "For at least some students," she wrote,

> the classroom has become a potentially traumatic environment, and they have begun to anticipate the emotional injuries they could suffer or inflict in a classroom conversation. They are also more inclined to insist that teachers protect them from causing or experiencing discomfort—and teachers in turn are more willing to oblige, because it would be considered injurious for them not to acknowledge a student's trauma or potential trauma.[45]

Gerson cites an instance recounted to her by a colleague, one of whose students asked her "not to use the word 'violate' in class—as in 'Does this conduct violate the law?'—because the word was triggering. Some students even suggested that rape law not be taught because of its potential to cause distress."[46] And in a case that has since been reversed, a professor at Crafton Hills College in California was required to add a trigger warning to his syllabus when a student and her parents complained about the "violent and pornographic content" of the graphic novels *Fun Home* and *Persepolis*, among others.[47] The Crafton Hills president reversed the injunction after reading the AAUP report on the topic.

That report clearly sums up the problems with trigger warnings:

> The presumption that students need to be protected rather than challenged in a classroom is at once infantilizing and anti-intellectual. It makes comfort a higher priority than intellectual engagement and . . . it singles out politically controversial topics like sex, race, class, capitalism and colonialism for attention. Indeed, if such topics are associated with triggers, correctly or not, they are likely to be marginalized if not avoided altogether by faculty who fear complaints for offending or discomforting some of their students. . . . Some discomfort is inevitable in classrooms if the goal is to expose students to new ideas, have them question beliefs they have taken for granted, grapple with ethical problems they have never considered, and more generally, expand their horizons so as to become informed and responsible democratic citizens. Trigger warnings suggest that classrooms should offer protection and comfort rather than an intellectually challenging education. They reduce students to vulnerable victims rather than full participants in the intellectual process of education. The effect is to stifle thought on the part of both teachers and students who fear to raise questions that might make others "uncomfortable."[48]

The importance of comfort has been highlighted by the recent expansion of the mandate of Title IX, the 1972 amendment to the Higher Education Act of 1965. Most of us associate Title IX with the opening to women of college athletic programs, and, indeed, that was its focus for many years, even though its language was much broader, outlawing discrimination based on sex in "any education program or activity receiving federal financial assistance." Since about 2010 the statute has been used increasingly to address sexual harassment, from one perspective a welcome addition to its mandate. For years feminists have insisted that sexual harassment is not simply annoying or inappropriate behavior, that rape is not merely a violent exception to the social relations of the sexes, that these are instead both symptoms and causes of gender inequality. The government's willingness to acknowledge these issues is, in principle, a positive development. But the approach, articulated in 2011 by the Office of Civil Rights of the Department of Education, shifted the emphasis from institutional inequalities to individual security. Of course, the law required demonstration of personal injury in claims about discrimination, but it seems to me that in the new regime the remedy has more to do with providing comfort and individual redress (with ridding the campus of a single perpetrator) than with addressing policies and institutions—personal injury, in other words, remains personal and the political dimension of it is lost. So when a student's claim that she has been raped is shown to be fabricated (as seems to have been the case at the University of Virginia in 2014), the entire problem seems to vanish even as the misogynist cultures remain intact.

The test for what counts as sexual harassment has also been expanded. It cited words that "may be harmful or humiliating," that may "limit" rather than prevent access to all the benefits an educational institution should provide. These changes were, in fact, minimal, but they were interpreted to widen the range of unacceptable words and actions. The notion of the hostile environment was expanded to include upsetting or unsettling ideas. In the process, the careful balance between First Amendment rights and the identification of unacceptable discrimination was upset, opening the way for all manner of "complaints against the expression of unpopular or controversial ideas." Joan Bertin, the executive director of the National Coalition Against Censorship, suggests that the Office of Civil Rights' efforts "to prevent discrimination [have] reached beyond what the enabling statutes—as interpreted by the Supreme Court—envisioned and [have] instead created a climate of fear on college and university campuses that not only threatens free speech and academic freedom, but also undermines the educational environment and the cause of equality."[49]

In its zeal to make campuses safer for students, the federal government weakened the standards for filing Title IX complaints: only one incident was necessary to initiate action instead of an earlier requirement that a pervasive or persistent pattern of discrimination must be proven to exist. And that one complaint was no longer subject to the criterion of "reasonable doubt"; all that there need be was "a preponderance of evidence" that some form of harassment has occurred. The government's requirement that schools take "prompt and effective action" to end harassment has led risk-averse university administrators who fear losing federal funds to bypass established procedures of due process, in many instances by dismissing alleged perpetrators with no trial whatsoever or by calling in outside investigators to prepare secret reports that are not shared with the accused.[50]

This is what happened in 2014 to Laura Kipnis, a professor of radio, TV, and film at Northwestern University. In response to an article she published in the *Chronicle Review* commenting critically (and often flippantly) on the rules about sexual contact between faculty and students at her university and in which she referred to an ongoing case (but with no names of those involved), some women students—who disagreed with her views—filed complaints under Title IX charging that her article had "a chilling effect" on their ability to report sexual misconduct. (Although Kipnis was not herself charged with any kind of sexual assault, the students carried mattresses and pillows—thereby identifying themselves as rape victims—when they protested her article.) When a colleague reported to the faculty senate on the interrogation of Kipnis by two outside legal investigators (although she was denied legal counsel, she was allowed to bring him as a support person to the interview), and when the university president wrote a piece in the *Wall Street Journal* on the dangers of the investigation to academic freedom, the same students filed Title IX complaints against them, charging "retaliation." Kipnis was eventually exonerated on the grounds that "the preponderance of evidence" did not support the complaints, but the questions raised by the way in which the charges were dealt with endure.[51] And not only at Northwestern. At Bard College, Title IX complaints led the university to instigate secret proceedings (the results of which were not initially shared with the professor charged) and to remove a professor from his position as the director of the chemistry program. At the University of Colorado, Patti Adler, a professor of sociology who taught a popular course titled "Deviance in U.S. Society," was charged by some students with sexual harassment for a skit on prostitution that was performed in her class. In the wake of the controversy, she resigned from her post.[52] At Louisiana State University, Teresa Buchanan, a tenured associate professor of education, was fired for using an occasional profanity in class. "Her alleged offense included saying, in class, 'fuck no' and making a joke about sex declining in long-term relationships, as well as using the word 'pussy' in an off-campus conversation with a teacher."[53] Although a faculty

committee recommended only censure in the light of her ster-
ling record, the president terminated her position—one she
had held for more than twenty years. (Buchanan unsuccessfully sued LSU; in 2018 the court upheld her firing.[54])

The charges against Kipnis came from self-designated feminists on the left; those against Adler and Buchanan, it seems,
from moral or religious conservatives who were offended by (as
one article on Buchanan put it) their "salty" speech. The quick
and ill-considered rush to judgment, by either Title IX administrators (a growing cadre of experts seeking to conform university policies to the law) or deans and presidents, downplays or
ignores issues of free speech in the name of compliance with federal mandates. The overarching goal of protecting victims or
potential victims fosters a combination of student vigilantism
and administrative risk aversion that has become a major threat
to the principles and practices of academic freedom.

These violations of academic freedom are not the only results
of the new interest the Department of Education has in dealing
with sexual harassment. At some universities there has been
important attention to the cultures of sports, fraternities, alco-
hol and drugs and to the ways in which these institutional cultures may undermine all attempts to secure gender equality. But
these efforts are compromised when the harassment is understood only as an individually perpetrated and individually experienced crime and not as part of a pattern of culturally sanctioned
behavior.

There are, in other words, uses and abuses of the expanded
applications of the Title IX legislation. The abuses personalize
and individualize what should be a structural analysis, and
they are symptomatic of the patterns of neoliberal rationality
that Brown has analyzed. As the university has become a site
for the development of individual human capital and no longer

the crucible for democratic citizenship, the state's role is to minimize impediments to economic success. (That also explains attention to skyrocketing student loans and to the corrupt practices of for-profit institutions, which impede the free market operations—not of ideas, but of capital accumulation.) The demands for social justice and equality of the 1960s have been turned into claims for the protection of individuals; attention to ethics has occluded issues of politics. In this way the ongoing Reagan revolution has coopted the social movements of the left.

WHAT IS TO BE DONE?

I have no nostalgia for the witch hunts of the 1950s, but at least then the political stakes were clear. The disturbing thing now is the evacuation of politics or, perhaps it's more accurate to say, the substitution of the politics of individual entitlement for the politics of collective equality and social justice. In the neoliberal university, comfort takes precedence over equality; wounded psyches over inegalitarian structures; and individual retribution or retaliation over challenges to the laws, institutions, and policies that perpetuate inequality. I'm the last person to say that psyches are irrelevant for understanding history, but it's not individual injury we need to interrogate (though that is surely one way inequality is felt). Rather, we need to investigate and challenge the deep material and psychic investments that allow injustices to persist, that justify unequal treatment in the name of immutable social norms, and that take (social, racial, ethnic, sexual, religious) differences to provide a natural explanation for hierarchy. That interrogation requires a kind of political consciousness that only critical thinking—of the sort universities were once supposed to encourage—can train us to do. Critical thinking thrives only in environments where academic freedom—the right to free and unfettered expression, however obnoxious and conflictual, and to faculty autonomy in curricular and pedagogical matters—is the guiding principle and practice for higher education. Bertin puts it clearly: "Educational institutions are the best places for young people to learn how to function in a pluralistic society. . . . Limiting the ability of students and faculty to discuss and debate the challenging issues of their time will leave them unprepared to make the kind of informed decisions required of participants in a representative democracy."[55] Critical thinking is uncomfortable and often disconcerting because it challenges the status quo; it needs academic freedom to secure and protect it.

Can academic freedom survive in the age of neoliberal civility? I'm not sure, and I don't have ready strategies to reclaim it; but I also can't imagine conceding that all is lost. Wendy Brown ends her book on neoliberal rationality with a call for the hard work of countering what she calls "civilizational despair," a sense of hopelessness in the face of the enormous global structures of power and inequality we now confront. It is particularly as teachers of the next generations and as believers in the importance of preserving democratic citizenship that her final sentence must resonate with us: "Yet what, apart from this work, could afford the slightest hope for a just, sustainable, and habitable future?"[56]

4

ACADEMIC FREEDOM
AND THE STATE

A cademic freedom is highly specific to institutions of scholarly research and teaching; it is not, like liberty or equality, a universal human right. It is not a general right of free speech, although the two are often confused. Instead academic freedom applies to those of us who are associated with universities. It refers both to the internal functions of the university—to the research and teaching that go on here—and to the external relations of the university with the nation-state.

It is the question of the relationship between the university and the state that I want to address. The relationship is not a simple one; it is traversed by tensions that are necessary and unresolvable. I will look at two of these tensions. The first is between the search for truth and the demands of power, what might be called a tension between *raison* and *raison d'état*. The second tension is between the hierarchical structure of the academy and the principles and practices of political democracies. I argue that academic freedom mediates both of these tensions.

THE UNIVERSITY AND THE NATION

The origin of the modern university has everything to do with nation-building. An older history is that of the religious sponsorship of universities, with the various relations between churches and states affecting their governance. Medieval universities were established to train priests, lawyers, doctors, and schoolmasters, not always with state sanction. It is Wilhelm von Humboldt who provided the model for the modern university at the University of Berlin early in the nineteenth century. One scholar describes its function this way: the Humboldtian university, he writes, "[is] the institution charged with watching over the spiritual life of the people of the rational state, reconciling ethnic tradition and statist rationality."[1] In Humboldt's vision, shared by many of his German idealist colleagues, the university's mission is to produce students committed to discovery and to inculcate the common language, history, literature, and geography that made possible the creation of a shared national culture. This unifying culture not only served a domestic function but also became an important arm of international competition and imperial expansion.

From the late eighteenth century on, there has been a tension between two avowed purposes of the university: to educate the citizens of the nation-state and, equally importantly, to encourage the critical thinking that would correct abuses of power and furnish the nation with the creativity and change that were vital to national well-being. Unfettered rational inquiry was taken to be the best guarantee of a healthy national future. This is Immanuel Kant's argument in "The Conflict of the Faculties" (1798).[2] There Kant insists that the faculty of philosophy (the so-called lower faculty) was the most vital arm of the university because its job was to interrogate the very foundations of the higher faculties of theology, medicine, and law. Philosophy's interrogation was a correction not only to stale disciplinary orthodoxy but also to the dangers of unfettered state power and its influence on those more practical disciplines. Kant's essay captures the dilemma that faced the modern university: how to reconcile reason and the state, the search for truth, and the requirements of power.[3] The literary scholar Masao Miyoshi describes this dilemma as a tension between "utilitarian nationalism" (the aim of which is to secure the national good) and "anti-utilitarian inquiry" (which depends on free and spontaneous expression). "The university as an institution has served Caesar and Mammon," he writes, "all the while manifesting its fealty to Minerva, Clio, and the Muses."[4]

This tension at the heart of the university's mission has been apparent throughout its history, although changes in demography and curriculum in the nations of the West have sometimes made it less apparent. Neoliberal transformations have certainly taken attention away from both national agendas and critical thinking: students are now more likely to be treated as paying clients, whose human capital can be enhanced by a university education and whose vocational interests should dictate the curriculum. The research and development needs of private companies more often drive the inquiries of professors (especially in the sciences), and globalization—not national interest—is at the heart of what some have called "the information and knowledge industry."[5] Still, I would argue that the Humboldt model has not entirely disappeared; its tensions remain as a legacy to be drawn on.

Those tensions have been clear in the postcolonial era, as new nations emerged to claim identities either denied or suppressed by imperial rule. Edward Said wrote compellingly of this process in a 1996 article titled "Identity, Authority, and Freedom."

There he points out, referring to developments in the Middle East, that "Arab universities are not only nationalist universities, but are also political institutions for perfectly understandable reasons."[6] This is understandable because "all societies accord a remarkable privilege to the university and school as crucibles for shaping national identity." Once national independence had freed these nations from the yokes of Ottoman or European imperialism, he noted, an opportunity opened to educate young people—to develop their pride—in the traditions, languages, history, and culture of their own countries. (The same might be said of the nations of Eastern and Central Europe after the end of Soviet rule in 1989.) But a terrible problem soon arose, Said notes, when national universities were "reconceived as extensions of the newly established national security state." As a result, the real value of education was short-circuited by the ruling party which sought "political conformity rather than intellectual excellence." "Nationalism in the university has come to represent not freedom but accommodation, not brilliance and daring but caution and fear, not the advancement of knowledge but self-preservation."[7] "Political repression," he goes on, "has never been good for academic freedom, and, perhaps, more importantly, it has been disastrous for academic and intellectual excellence."[8] The two—academic freedom and intellectual excellence—are, of course, entirely interdependent.

Without wanting to deny the importance of education for the construction of national identity, Said asks "which national identity?" and how might it be understood in relation to academic freedom? His answer—which I quote at length because I cannot match its clarity and eloquence—acknowledges the needs of the nation but makes critical intellectual work its own raison d'être. "My assessment of Arab academic life is that too high a price has been paid in sustaining nationalist regimes that have allowed political passions and an ideology of conformity to dominate—perhaps even to swallow up—civil institutions such as the university. To make the practice of intellectual discourse dependent on conformity to a predetermined political ideology is to nullify intellect altogether."[9] For Said, intellectual discourse is, above all, "the freedom to be critical: criticism *is* intellectual life and, while the academic precinct contains a great deal in it, its spirit is intellectual and critical, and neither reverential nor patriotic."[10] It is the freedom to critique the terms of an exclusionary national identity that is vital both to the university and the nation, "Otherwise, I fear, the old inequities, cruelties, and unthinking attachments that have so disfigured human history will be recycled by the academy, which then loses much of its real intellectual freedom as a result."[11] Here, in a somewhat different language, is Kant's idea that critical philosophy provides the ultimate corrective to abuses of state power.

Said's notion of national identity is one that disclaims the triumph of one people over another and the insistence on homogeneity as the bottom line of a common culture. Instead, it is the recognition—enabled by critical thinkers in the humanities and social sciences especially—of its relation to other national identities and, within the nation, to the multiple identities we inhabit, to the differences that bind us, to a commonality of shared differences rather than to a genetic or historical sameness. Even more important is the lesson "that human life and history are secular— that is actually constructed and reproduced by men and women."[12] This means that there is nothing fixed about our social and political arrangements, that they are open to criticism and to change. It is precisely the specter of change, of course, that threatens the rulers of the authoritarian state.

Said argues that the function of academic freedom is to protect and preserve the critical spirit, ensuring the pursuit of justice and truth wherever it might lead. "Rather than viewing the search for knowledge in the academy as the search for coercion and control over others, we should regard knowledge as something for which to *risk* identity, and we should think of academic freedom as an invitation to give up on identity in the hope of understanding and perhaps even assuming more than one."[13]

ACADEMIC FREEDOM

"Our model for academic freedom," Said writes, "should be the migrant or traveler," voyaging beyond familiar places, confronting the unknown.[14] For him, academic freedom is a kind of passport for international travel—guaranteeing the right of scholars to go wherever the search for truth may lead. It was one way of addressing the tension at the heart of the mission of the modern university—that between utilitarian nationalism and nonutilitarian inquiry, between reason of state and reason itself.

In the United States, the concept of academic freedom was formulated by a group of professors at the turn of the last century precisely as a way of mediating that tension, of providing a rationale for an autonomous faculty, not as a peculiar elitist privilege but as a guarantee of advancing "the common good." In 1915 the newly organized American Association of University Professors (AAUP; among its founders is the American pragmatist John Dewey), articulated a vision of the university that was at once immune to powerful interests (in the United States, these were both state legislators and private benefactors—Caesar and Mammon) and that promised to serve them, however indirectly, by producing new knowledge for the common good. Their version of academic freedom rested on the notion that knowledge and power are separable: the pursuit of truth ought to have nothing to do with public conflicts of interest, even if new knowledge could weigh in on one side or another of those conflicts. The university was defined as "an inviolable refuge from [the] tyranny [of public opinion] . . . an intellectual experiment station, where new ideas may germinate and where their fruit, though distasteful to the community as a whole, may be allowed to ripen."[15] As that last reference to "distasteful" reactions indicates, academic freedom was designed to protect the most critical, the most unorthodox of university faculty. A professor ought to be "a contagious center of intellectual enthusiasm," wrote one university president. "It is better for students to think about heresies than not to think at all; better for them to climb new trails and stumble over error if need be, than to ride forever in upholstered ease on the overcrowded highway."[16]

The best statement I have seen of the principle of academic freedom comes from the regents of the University of Wisconsin in 1894, repudiating efforts by the state superintendent of education to fire Professor Richard T. Ely, who, among other things, had published a book on socialism.[17]

> As Regents of a university with over a hundred instructors supported by nearly two millions of people who hold a vast diversity of views regarding the great questions which at present agitate the human mind, we could not for a moment think of recommending the dismissal or even the criticism of a teacher even if some of his opinions should, in some quarters, be regarded as visionary. Such a course would be equivalent to saying that no professor should teach anything which is not accepted by everybody as true. This would cut our curriculum down to very small proportions. We cannot for a moment believe that knowledge has reached its final goal, or that the present condition of society is perfect. We must therefore welcome from our teachers such

discussions as shall suggest the means and prepare the way by which knowledge may be extended, present evils be removed and others prevented. We feel that we would be unworthy of the position we hold if we did not believe in progress in all departments of knowledge. In all lines of academic investigation it is of the utmost importance that the investigator should be absolutely free to follow the indications of truth wherever they may lead. Whatever may be the limitations which trammel inquiry elsewhere we believe the great state University of Wisconsin should ever encourage that continual and fearless sifting and winnowing by which alone the truth can be found.[18]

The autonomy of professors defended in this statement rested on the fact that the faculty was a self-regulating body, trained and credentialed according to the rules of their discipline and profession. They were, in the words of the philosopher John Dewey, "an organized society of truth-seekers" uniquely qualified to judge one another's abilities.[19] These organized societies were the national professional associations that trained and certified competence, a form of expertise we depend on for the advancement of knowledge in all fields. The legal scholar Robert Post puts it this way: "Disciplines are grounded on the premise that some ideas are better than others; disciplinary communities claim the prerogative to discriminate between competent and incompetent work."[20] University administrators (those charged with the efficient running of the institution and its legal and financial operations) and trustees (who govern with ultimate authority) are not in a position to question the expertise of the faculty in matters of research and teaching; instead they share governance with the faculty, each carrying responsibility for separate activities, together ensuring the viability of the institution. The guarantee of academic freedom is at the heart of their relationship.

I was reminded as I wrote this of an experience I had at the Central European University more than 15 years ago, during the tumultuous reign of the rector Yehuda Elkana. At one meeting that I attended, he confronted faculty and students who were protesting the planned reform or elimination of programs in gender studies and environmental studies. There he justified his right to decide unilaterally with a phrase that was endlessly ridiculed by those who considered him something of a tyrant. "A university is not a democracy," he said. In a way, of course, he was right. But not exactly. Typically, a university is not a democracy in the sense that everyone gets to vote about what is taught and how (although there are exceptions, I'm told—for example, in the Cambridge colleges in the United Kingdom)—but more typically, it is a hierarchically organized cooperative society, perhaps better to say a federation, of experts with different competencies and who share responsibility for its critical social mission. Trustees usually have the final say, and administrators recommend action about faculty and students to them. But a certain division of labor is also the norm. Ideally, each group should respect the others' competencies in their processes of decision-making. Of course, the dangers of trustee or administrative overreach are sometimes as troubling as interference from politicians and financial patrons, but so are calls from the Right (we are hearing lots of this in the United States these days) for students' right of free speech to determine what is taught and for "substantive neutrality" or balanced interpretations in the classroom. Post's reply to this movement seems right to me: "Disciplines do not create expert knowledge through a market place of ideas in which content discrimination is prohibited and all ideas are deemed equal."[21] Although there are often conflicts within disciplines about what counts as acceptable work—critical new ideas are not always granted validity, and there have been long struggles by scholars (feminists, post-structuralists, critical race theorists, queer theorists) to achieve legitimacy for their fields of study—still it is academic freedom and not student free speech that informs these struggles.

If academic freedom is the prerogative of a specialized group of professional intellectuals, and if the university in which they work is not technically a democracy, on what basis can the university claim its rights? Why is it that academic freedom has been the cry of university presidents and faculty facing unprecedented attacks by authoritarian politicians in Turkey, Poland, Hungary, and, lately, the United States?

It may be paradoxical to argue that democracy depends on the university even if the university is not itself a perfect democracy. But that is the case. It is the case because critical thinking—Kant's notion of reason in the face of power, or Dewey's idea that innovation depends on challenging "deep-rooted prejudice," or Said's insistence that "freedom cannot simply be reduced to venerating the unexamined authority of a national identity and its culture"—critical thinking is the lifeblood of democratic societies; without it, all visions of justice and hope are lost.[22] Critical thinking depends on informed and disciplined knowledge, on our ability to search for—and to teach our students *how* to search for—truth. That kind of teaching is not a democratic process; it cannot be one. And yet democracy depends on it. (Real democracy, I should add. Hungarian prime minister Viktor Orbán's notion of "illiberal democracy" is an oxymoron.)

When the state finds itself at odds with critical thinking, we know the search for truth has been shut down; when populist orators decry the elitism of the academic establishment, we know knowledge production is being directed to nefarious ends; when what Said called the "secular" dimension of critique (its refusal of transcendent explanations for human life, whether based on

history, god, or nature) is replaced by invocations of essential-
ism, we know the borders of knowledge are being closed and the
search for truth, in whatever realm, is canceled. The denial of
academic freedom to its universities, of permission to pursue
truth wherever it leads, signals the ultimate failure of democracy. And it does not bode well for the future prosperity and
health of the nation.

PUBLIC AND PRIVATE

One of the ironies of the current relationship between universities and nations is that the most endangered institutions are the
ones once considered the most democratic—the public universities supported by the state. Those universities that are open to
students at minimal tuition costs depend on the state for financial support, but legally the state also has ultimate authority to
determine their future. Indeed, it is often in the name of protecting the public's financial interest that politicians usually justify their intervention in curricular and faculty domains. This has
been the case at the University of Wisconsin since the election
of the right-wing Republican governor, Scott Walker. He has
dismantled institutions of faculty governance and tenure and has
eliminated humanities and social sciences programs at many sat-
ellite campuses in the name of cost efficiency and vocational
training.[23] It is the publicly funded universities that most easily
succumb to the demand that (as Said put it) "intellectual discourse must worship at the altar of national identity," and so
succumb to the suppression of critical inquiry that is the inevitable result.[24]

The resurgence of strong nationalist tendencies is evident
across the world, at least in part, as a reaction to the rise of

globalization and its undermining of the frontiers of national sovereignty. The reassertion of the importance of the nation is arguably the populist response to the crisis of neoliberal capitalism.

In the modern period, new private universities have grown alongside public ones, often to represent special interests that weren't being served adequately in the public realm. The numbers of the new private universities vary widely from country to country, as does their relationship to the state. Usually there is some kind of contractual agreement that recognizes their legitimacy as degree-granting institutions, but they tend to have greater independence than their public counterparts. In the United States, as elsewhere, many private universities were originally founded by religious groups, but that was not exclusively the case. And even those that were originally religious have become increasingly secular, as is the case with the American universities in Cairo and Beirut. Some private universities were established to provide a more elite environment for students of the upper classes or for those with financial means but who were ineligible for admission to public schools. Although private universities typically require state certification, they are less susceptible to direct intervention than are state-supported institutions whose financial interest gives the state greater power to intervene.

That is why the private institutions have been able to preserve something of the critical spirit in the face of all-out assaults on higher education by those seeking to consolidate nationalist identities and to eliminate not just opposition but the kind of thinking that would call rulers to account for the violations of principle and justice they undertake. Of course, private universities are subject to pressures from donors and politicians— they are not immune from attempts to rein in critique and to control what is studied. Nor are they free of the neoliberal processes that are everywhere undermining the substance and ethos of a classical university education. But, still, they occupy a privileged place in the realm of academe and that privilege has made them, in our time, the custodians of academic freedom in the sense I have been talking about it—as the protection of the search for truth wherever it leads, of the spirit of critical inquiry that, at its best, refuses compromise.

If, in the United States, the University of Wisconsin is no longer a place that allows for the "continual and fearless sifting and winnowing by which alone the truth can be found," private institutions remain in a better position to promote that legacy. It is on their campuses that it is still possible to teach freely and to resist interference—the call for academic freedom resonates with the values and principles to which they at least nominally aspire.

I think that is the case for the Central European University in Hungary. As the only private institution of higher education in the nation, it has long been able to stand apart from the currents and passions of successive political regimes. It has also long been a training ground for the leadership of movements for social justice, the rule of law, and the creation of open societies in the region. On the one hand, one might ask how a small graduate institution could pose a serious threat to a government with vast military and police resources at its disposal. On the other hand, the fact of the attack signals the danger that the quest for truth by critical thinkers is seen to pose to authoritarian rule. The frightening aspect of this is that power is on the side of the state. Indeed, the resolution of the crisis might well come from a negotiation between two sovereign entities—the state of New York and the nation of Hungary!

But there is also a hopeful side to the story. It suggests that, despite the lamentations of scholars about the end of the university as we knew it, there is something that persists against great odds.[25] The process of erosion of the academy has been gradual and incomplete, allowing the legacy of Kant and Humboldt to survive even as its homogenizing cultural function has disappeared. There are pockets of resistance on campuses that honor the principles and practices of truth seeking. We can see this in the calls for academic freedom that echo across the globe, in the thousands of protestors who filled the streets of Budapest and who also continue to speak out in Turkey, Poland, and the United States. We can see it in the international outcry against intellectual repression that refuses to accept defeat. And, perhaps ironically, we can see it, too, in the determination of authoritarian rulers to banish critical thought and the institutions that foster it. Their determination is a measure of the aspirational power of the idea of academic freedom, but it is only aspirational. To get rulers to value and respect academic freedom requires a political struggle, the dimensions of which are extremely large.

What is the nature of that political struggle? Does it undermine the pluralism and diversity of views that are the proud values of the search for truth and the production of knowledge? I don't think so. The protection of critical thinking has always involved a confrontation with power. By its very nature, it is political. The political struggle I am referring to is not partisan or ideological; rather, it commits us to the continued practice of critical thinking. The principle that guides us, that articulates the meaning of our struggle, is academic freedom. Critical thinking, in this definition of it, is both the cause and effect of academic freedom.

I leave you, then, with a circular argument: we need academic freedom to protect the necessarily nonpartisan but nonetheless political work of critical thinking even as we must engage in that political/intellectual work to bring academic freedom to life. But the politics of the moment requires more than critical thinking; it requires rallying support for the only guarantee we have that democracy can be saved or restored. This means we need to think and act on that requirement: to recognize the importance (to say nothing of the pleasure) of our intellectual work and to find the practical political means to continue to do it. It is the challenge we urgently face, and one we have no choice but to meet.

5

ON FREE SPEECH AND
ACADEMIC FREEDOM

I was ten years old when my father was suspended from his job as a high school social studies teacher. Two years later, he was fired for insubordination and conduct unbecoming a teacher because he refused to cooperate with an investigation into purported communist infiltration in the New York City public schools.[1] At the time, I took it all in stride—we were expected to be proud of the principled stand my father had taken. But looking back, I can see that I was also afraid. Our family life was rendered uncertain by his firing and not only because he no longer had a job. In fact, it was not so much economic insecurity that I felt but a sense of foreboding: FBI agents showing up at the door, friends whose fathers were in jail, Joseph McCarthy's voice leering, insinuating, angry—sounds that to a child conveyed dangerous, unreasoning hatred.

That was some sixty-five years ago. I thought all of it was long passed, a stage in my history—in American history—a stage we had all survived and that even some of its most ardent supporters had repudiated. So I was unprepared for the power of my reaction to the election of Donald Trump: diffuse anxiety; a sense of foreboding in response to an indeterminate threat; dread about what would come next, as day after day more draconian measures were announced. It was, in some sense, the return of the repressed and not only for me but for the country.

Looking for insight, I turned (not for the first time) to Richard Hofstadter's *Anti-Intellectualism in American Life*, a reflection on the experience of the 1950s, published from the critical distance of 1966. In the book's first chapter, Hofstadter comments on "the national disrespect for mind" that characterized the era. "Primarily it was McCarthyism which aroused the fear that the critical mind was at a ruinous discount in this country. Of course, intellectuals were not the only targets of McCarthy's constant detonations—he was after bigger game—but intellectuals were in the line of fire, and it seemed to give special rejoicing to his followers when they were hit."[2] Hofstadter went on to argue that the experience of the 1950s was not new but a recurrent aspect of American identity with "a long historical background. An examination of this background suggests that regard for intellectuals in the United States has not moved steadily downward . . . but is subject to cyclical fluctuations."[3] My son, Tony, characterized these fluctuations as the escape of the American id from the confines of its reasonable containment. The return of the repressed with a vengeance!

The American id has been let loose again, this time by Donald Trump, and, as in the McCarthy period, intellectuals are only one of his targets. But targets we are. It's not only the president's preference for alternative facts that challenge evidence-based argument but direct attacks by him and others on scientists who work on climate change or who challenge drug company claims about the safety of their products. It's also an apparent distrust of and dislike for writers, artists, journalists, and professors. Secretary of Education Betsy DeVos tells college students that "the fight against the education establishment extends to you too. The faculty, from adjunct professor to deans, tell you what to do, what to say, and more ominously what to think."[4] We are, in her view, dangerous agents of thought control, purveying our ideology to the detriment of free thought. A "Professor Watchlist," established by the conservative organization Turning Point USA, publishes online the "names of professors that advance a radical agenda in lecture halls."[5] An Arizona legislator introduced a bill that would prohibit state institutions from offering any class or activity that promotes "division, resentment or social justice toward a race, gender, religion, political affiliation, social class or other class of people." The bill failed, but it is a sign of the times. (Arizona has already banned the teaching of ethnic studies in grades K–12.[6]) In Arkansas another bill seeks to prohibit any writing by or about the Left historian Howard Zinn from inclusion in the school curriculum.[7] In Iowa a state senator introduced a bill to use political party affiliation as a test for faculty appointments. "A person shall not be hired as a . . . member of the faculty . . . if the person's political party affiliation . . . would cause the percentage of faculty belonging to one political party to exceed by ten percent the percentage of faculty belonging to the other party."[8] A Republican Party operative in Michigan revealed his darker side in a tweet recalling the Kent State shootings of students protesting the Vietnam War and recommends similar treatment for today's demonstrators: "Violent protestors who shut down free speech? Time for another Kent State perhaps. One bullet stops a lot of thuggery."[9] The *New York Times* cites a report by the Anti-Defamation League noting that since January 2016, white supremacists have stepped up recruiting on campuses in more than thirty states.[10] Their anti-Semitic, anti-Muslim leaflets have caused concern but also—as in the case of speeches by the likes of white nationalist Richard Spencer or the *Breitbart* provocateur Milo Yiannopoulos—they have raised the question of what counts as free speech.

These days free speech is the mantra of the Right, their weapon in the new culture war. Their invocation of free speech has collapsed an important distinction between the First Amendment right of free speech that we all enjoy and the principle of academic freedom that refers to teachers and the knowledge they produce and convey. In a recent article, the legal scholar Robert Post clarifies the distinction between the two. The First Amendment, he writes, consists of three core rules that apply to public discourse: i) the state is prohibited from regulating speech; ii) the expression of all ideas is permitted (there is no such thing as a 'false' idea); and iii) restraints on "the voluntary public expression of ideas" are prohibited.[11] He points out that classic First Amendment doctrine "cannot apply to 'speech as such,'" but only to that which seeks to express or inform public opinion.[12] It is when we are acting as "sovereign agents of self-government" that we are protected by the First Amendment.[13] Post insists, as well, that it is questionable whether the First Amendment applies to any speech at a university since the education of students does not assume them to be such sovereign agents. Nor do professors have an unfettered right of free speech in the classroom—they are constrained by the need to teach their subject matter; their job as educators limits their rights of free speech. They do, however, have academic freedom. "The scope of academic freedom is not determined by First Amendment principles of freedom of speech, but by the metrics of professional competence. Professor are free to teach in ways that are regarded as professionally competent."[14] It is disciplinary associations that train and certify this competence, a form of expert knowledge we depend on for the advancement of knowledge in all fields. Post puts it this way: "Disciplines are grounded on the premise that some ideas are better than others; disciplinary communities claim the prerogative to discriminate between competent and incompetent work."

And "disciplines do not create expert knowledge through a market place of ideas in which content discrimination is prohibited and all ideas are deemed equal."[15]

These days the Right's reference to free speech sweeps away guarantees of academic freedom, dismissing as so many violations of the Constitution the thoughtful, critical articulation of ideas; the demonstration of proof based on rigorous examination of evidence; the distinction between true and false, between careful and sloppy work; the exercise of reasoned judgment. Their free speech means the right to one's opinion, however unfounded, however ungrounded, and it extends to every venue, every institution. The Goldwater Institute's model legislation, the "Campus Free Speech Act," has been taken up in Tennessee and North Dakota and by the National Association of Scholars. It calls on professors to present both sides of an issue in the classroom in order to protect the student right of free speech. A teacher, in this view, has the right to regulate speech, "provided that [he or she] regulates the speech in a viewpoint- and content-neutral manner."[16] In effect, students are allowed to say anything they want, removing intellectual authority from the professor. Here is the vice president of the College Republicans at the University of Tennessee supporting a bill to protect student free speech: "Students are often intimidated by the academic elite in the classroom. Tennessee is a conservative state, we will not allow out of touch professors with no real-world experience to intimidate eighteen-year-olds."[17] The National Association of Scholars has proposed new ways to evaluate the "academic elite." Among their recommendations is the elimination of peer review and its replacement by "experts" "who are of genuinely independent minds."[18] It's hard not to see in these recommendations a more veiled version of the political party test proposed by the Iowa legislator.

There's a kind of blood lust evident in these charges, an attempt to rein in serious intellectual work, critical thinking, scientific inquiry. I don't want to deny problems on "our" side: the moralism that is apparent in some courses and some student activism, the calls for "trigger warnings," the insistence on the authority of their experiences by those whose minority status has silenced or marginalized them—who look to "safe spaces" as a way to gain traction in an otherwise hostile or neglectful institutional and social environment, who erupt in protests that are sometimes ill-considered violations of the rights they need to respect and protect. But these don't explain the ferocity of the anti-intellectualism we are witnessing, the desire to impugn our motives and disparage our work, to do away with what power academics are supposed to have. If Tony's reference to the unleashed id is right, we are the superego who would spoil the fun, who endanger its unruly pursuits. We keep asking questions; they already know the answers. We have to be gotten rid of if they are to enjoy their power to its fullest—because that power depends on reversing advances to equality that have been made and undermining the institutions of democracy: the Constitution, the citizenry, the courts, and the schools. These are the institutions of government that, arguably, provide the ground rules for the conflict and diversity that James Madison understood to be the permanent condition of the republic. In his view of it, regulation is the guarantee of democracy.

That may be why freedom is the principle invoked so forcefully on the right these days—freedom in the sense of the absence of any restraint. From this perspective, the bad boys can say anything they want, however vile and hateful: Yiannopoulos, Spencer, Charles Murray, Donald Trump. The worse the better, for it confirms their masculine prowess, their ability to subvert

the dogmas of political correctness, to laugh away the school-
marmish moralism of those they designate "eggheads" and
"snowflakes"—female-identified prudes who, in a certain ste-
reotypical rendering of mothers, wives, and girlfriends, are the
killjoys who seek to rein in the aggressive, unfettered sexuality
that is the mark of their manly power. Intellectuals and liberals
(the terms are often taken to be synonymous) are portrayed as
enemies of this freedom. "Inside every liberal is a totalitarian
screaming to get out," warns David Horowitz, who has been on
the front lines of the anti-intellectual movement for years.[19] The
strategy of the alt-right these days is to provoke situations that
can be used to demonstrate the truth of Horowitz's claim. By
collapsing the distinction between free speech and academic
freedom, they deny the authority of knowledge and of the teacher
who purveys it. The political scientist Danielle Allen fell into
their trap when she compared Charles Murray's experience at
Middlebury College last March (protesters prevented him from
speaking) with that of the Little Rock Nine, the black high
school students who had to be protected from violent crowds by
the National Guard as they sought to integrate Central High
School in Arkansas in 1957. In her rendering of it, the proponent
of racist, false science becomes, surprisingly, the defender of "the
intellectual life of democracies." Like the Little Rock Nine, who
defied racists and "tried, simply, to go to school," she concludes,
"Murray and his hosts were also trying, simply, to keep school
open. In this moment, they, too, were heroes."[20]

Middlebury, I would submit, was not about "the intellectual
life of democracies"—that goes on in schools and forums where
tests of truth and evidence apply. It *was* about the violation of
an individual's right of free speech, where no such standards are
applied. (But if we take Post's view, that there was no educational

function performed by Murray's speech, we might also argue that the invitation to him contradicted the university's stated mission.[21])

The confusion between academic freedom and free speech was evident in the call for respect for individuals with different points of view, issued in the wake of Middlebury, by the unlikely duo of Harvard democratic socialist Cornel West and Princeton conservative Robert George.[22] As they insist on the importance of respecting free speech, their statement also concedes what should be refused: the conflation between the individual's right to express his opinions and criticism—lack of respect, even—for the opinions themselves. West and George assume a necessary parity between different sides of the debates about discrimination, equality, and justice as well as about what counts as scientific evidence and the validity of certain forms of political protest. The issue of the authority of knowledge is denied in their calls for neutrality, as is the unequal distribution of social power; it is as if everything is of the same quality in the marketplace of ideas.

Free speech makes no distinction about quality; academic freedom does. Are all opinions equally valid in a university classroom? Does creationism trump science in the biology curriculum if half the students believe in it? Do both sides carry equal weight in the training of future scientists? Are professors being "ideological" when they refuse to accept biblical accounts as scientific evidence? What then becomes of certified professorial expertise? Does the university have a responsibility to uphold standards of truth seeking outside the classroom as well as inside it? When does an invitation imply endorsement of a speaker's views? What is the difference between a climate-change denier and a Holocaust denier? Is the exchange of ideas really impeded by passionate debate, even angry exclamations? Ought the right of free speech be restricted to polite and reasonable exposition?

Is righteous anger unreasonable in the face of racial, economic, religious, or sexual discrimination? Is there really no difference between the structures of discrimination experienced by African Americans and the criticism of those structures leveled against whites? Are both worthy of being deemed racist, as the conservative student newspaper at Pitzer College claimed?[23] Does "all lives matter" carry the same critical commentary as "black lives matter?" What has it meant historically for those marginalized by or excluded from majority conversations and institutions to protest their treatment? Sometimes it requires extraordinary actions to make one's voice heard in a conversation that routinely ignores it. Incivility, even today, is most often a charge made against protesters on the left, while the hate speech of those on the right looks for—and finds—protection in the right of free speech.

Although there are differences between reactions to student protest and the more general defamation of the life of the mind that targets faculty, there are also connections between them. These have to do with the status of criticism or critique in the national conversation. It was in defense of the university's role as the crucible of critique that the doctrine of academic freedom was formulated in the United States over a century ago. When John Dewey and his colleagues founded the American Association of University Professors in 1915, they articulated a vision of academia that was at once immune to powerful economic and political interests and that promised to serve those interests, however indirectly, by producing new knowledge "for the common good."[24]

The century-old notion of academic freedom insists on the expertise of scholars and the importance of that expertise for advancing "the common good." The same notion of the relationship between knowledge and the common good inspired the founding in 1780 of the American Academy of Arts and Sciences. "The Arts and Sciences," the charter of incorporation reads, "are necessary to the wealth, peace, independence and happiness of a people."[25] "From its beginnings," the academy's current history notes, "the Academy has engaged in the critical questions of the day. It has brought together the nation's and the world's most distinguished citizens to address social and intellectual issues of common concern and above all, to develop ways to translate knowledge into action."[26]

The academy's mandate, like the principle of academic freedom is, to be sure, full of so-called elitist implications—intellectuals in general, and the faculty in particular, are corporate, self-regulating (disciplined) bodies whose training to produce new knowledge guarantees a certain autonomy and a share in the governance of the university and the regard of the nation. This is not elitism but expertise, the production of knowledge informed by disciplined research, science in the public interest. Post puts it nicely, "We depend on doctors to create vaccines to immunize us against Zika; we rely upon engineers to build bridges. We do not crowdsource such questions or decide them by public opinion polls or by popular vote."[27] I would add that the same goes for knowledge of the law and legal precedent and for the history and sociology of race, gender, sexuality, and class.

In this view, the faculty is capable of inspiring, inculcating, and judging student mastery of subjects being taught. Student free speech is appropriately limited in the university classroom, subject to the disciplinary tutelage of the professor in charge—a professor who has been subjected to and certified by a disciplined formation of his or her own. This does not mean silent acquiescence in the face of indoctrination—far from it. It does mean learning how to critically evaluate things, how to question orthodoxy and challenge it from a position of knowledge rather than one of unexamined belief. This training in the rigors of critical thought is not without its difficulties, and it is more often characterized by strong differences and contentious argument than it is by consensus and singular conclusions. But that is what makes it the preparation required for the exercise—inside and outside the classroom—of free speech. Academic freedom—the right of teachers to teach as they choose, without outside inter-ference—is, I argue, the key to the exercise of free speech. Free speech not as the expression of the unruly id but as the voice given to reasoned argument. That voice can be angry, insistent, condemnatory; there is no contradiction between reason and outrage.

That is why exhorting students to respect the ideas of indi-viduals with whom they disagree is not the solution to their pur-ported misbehavior: we can respect the rights of free speech without having to respect the ideas being uttered. Critical think-ing is precisely not a program of neutrality, not tolerance of all opinion, not an endorsement of the idea that anything goes. It is about how one brings knowledge to bear on criticism; it is a procedure, a method that shapes and disciplines thought. This kind of critical thinking has been discouraged in university class-rooms in recent years; it has been severely compromised as the mission of the university, replaced by an emphasis on vocational preparation, on the comfort and security of students, on the avoidance of controversy lest students, parents, trustees, legisla-tors, and donors find offense. Its absence in the university curriculum has produced some of the problems we now face.

The lack of training in critical thinking extends beyond sub-ject matter in courses to strategic planning for political action. If students haven't learned how to analyze texts and histori-cal arguments, they won't be able to bring critical thinking to political engagements; they will tend to act more impulsively, venting their rage rather than directing it to considered strategic ends. They will underestimate the power of the opposition to discredit their aims along with their actions. They will end up—as in the Middlebury case—the bad guys while the racism of Charles Murray that they were legitimately protesting is eclipsed by his First Amendment martyrdom.

I know it's unfashionable to look to the past for answers to the present, unrealistic not to pragmatically accept the corporate neoliberal university as a *fait accompli.* But I want to end this essay by suggesting there is some value in conserving the principles that inaugurated our democracy and informed the articulation of the mission of the colleges and universities of this country. If the production of knowledge was understood to be vital for the progress of the nation and the guarantee of "the wealth, peace, independence and happiness of [the] people," then intellectualism is our best answer to anti-intellectualism. Not the watering down of ideas or the search for popular consensus, not the notion that all ideas are worthy of respect, but the more difficult task of honing our critical capabilities, cultivating them in our students, and insisting on their value even in the face of ridicule, harassment, and repression.

In 1954 Leslie Fiedler described McCarthyism as a "psychological disorder compounded of the sour dregs of populism [and] the fear of excellence, difference and culture."[28] It's time, I think, to reassert excellence and the authority of knowledge in the face of the Trump administration's attempt to elevate mediocrity to a heroic virtue. The pursuit of knowledge is not an elitist activity but a practice vital for the exercise of democracy and the promotion of the common good. Those values—knowledge, democracy, and the common good—seem to me worth reasserting, even in the face of their corruption and neglect. The university was once considered the crucible of those values; its mission has been severely compromised over the course of the last twenty or thirty years. Still, we have no choice but to hold on to that vision and to find ways to reanimate it so that it can inspire our thinking in the difficult days that lie ahead.

IN THE AGE OF TRUMP,
A CHILLING ATMOSPHERE

An Interview with Joan Wallach Scott

BILL MOYERS

Back in the 1930s a scholarly intramural feud to choose the inscription for the new library at my future alma mater, the University of Texas at Austin, ended in a draw. From many nominations the competition came down to two finalists. Both said the same thing in different tongues: "Ye Shall Know the Truth and the Truth Shall Make You Free," from the biblical Gospel of John, and its Latin counterpart: "Cognoscetis Ventatem et veritas liberabit vos."

Fortunately—at least for me—the selection committee chose English. As I crossed that plaza as a student in the 1950s, and twice later when I spoke at commencement, I would look up (mainly to check the time on the huge clock high on the iconic tower rising above the library), catch a glimpse of the inscription, and be grateful that so many of my professors had fought hard to prevent the politically appointed Board of Regents from dictating exactly what truth could be taught. Some paid a dear price for defending academic freedom, among them survivors of a ferocious campaign waged the previous decade by the state legislature to fire the university president, a political assault bravely resisted by many faculty and students alike.

Attacks on the academy at large occur frequently in America, and never more intensely than now. Just consider these items from the news:

- A Republican legislator in Arizona introduced a bill that would prohibit state colleges from offering any class that promotes "division, resentment or social justice" without defining what he means by those words—Arizona earlier banned the teaching of ethnic studies in grades K–12.
- A Republican state senator in Iowa introduced a bill to use political party affiliation as a test for faculty appointments to colleges and universities.
- A Republican legislator in Arkansas filed a bill to ban any writing by or about the progressive historian Howard Zinn, author of the popular *A People's History of the United States.*
- In Wisconsin, Republican governor Scott Walker tried to remove all references to the university's commitment to the "search for truth."
- Wisconsin's Republican legislature has stripped state workers and professors of their collective bargaining rights for professors.
- Donald Trump's secretary of education, Betsy DeVos, has called on conservative college students to join the fight against the education establishment.
- A leader of the College Republicans at the University of Tennessee wants to protect students in the classroom from intimidation by "the academic elite." He announced that "Tennessee is a conservative state. We will not allow out-of-touch professors with no real-world experience to intimidate 18-year-olds."

- The right-wing organization Turning Point USA created a "professor watch list" and has been publishing online the names of professors "that advance a radical agenda in lecture halls."

No one I know has followed this trail with keener interest or deeper concern than Joan Wallach Scott, one of the most respected and influential scholars of our time. Professor Emerita in the School of Social Science at the Institute for Advanced Study in Princeton, she has been praised for groundbreaking work in feminist and gender theory, celebrated as a mentor, and honored as the author of several books; her latest, *Sex and Secularism*, will be published this fall. Earlier this year the American Academy of Arts and Sciences awarded her the Talcott Parsons Prize for distinguished contributions to the social sciences; previous recipients included Clifford Geertz in anthropology; C. Vann Woodward in history; Albert Hirschman in economics; and Daniel Kahneman in psychology.

BILL MOYERS: Professor Scott, connect these dots for us. What's the pattern?

JOAN SCOTT: The pattern is an attack on the university as a place where critical thinking occurs, where free thought is encouraged. This is not new, it's been going on for a number of years. It can be seen in the defunding of state universities. It can be seen in attacks on free speech at the university, particularly on the supposed tenured "radicals" who are teaching in universities. The Trump election brought it the fore and made it possible for a number of different groups whose aim is to stop the teaching of critical thinking to launch direct attacks.

MOYERS: You've said there's a kind of bloodlust evident at work. What do you mean by that?

SCOTT: Richard Hofstadter, in his famous book which was written in the time of the McCarthy period in the 1950 and 1960s, *Anti-intellectualism in American Life*, talks about the deep hatred that some Americans had for what they consider to be elitist intellectual activity. I think that's what's happening now—the vicious unleashing of attacks on professors and students, the clear decision by the Right to make free speech their campaign and to demonstrate that universities and particularly students are dangerous leftists who would deny to others the right of free speech. The Right as the victim of the intolerant Left. It is a concerted plan to depict the university itself as a place of dogmatic ideological thinking—an institution somehow out of step with the way most Americans think. What I mean by bloodlust is a kind of vicious vindictive description of the universities and their faculties.

For example, you read that quote from Betsy DeVos. She was warning students that they don't have to be indoctrinated by professors at their universities. But the reason you go to university is to be taught, is to learn how to think more clearly, to call into question the ideas that you came with and think about whether or not they are the ideas you will always want to hold. A university education at its best is a time of confusion and questioning, a time to learn how to think clearly about the values and principles that guide one's life. Of course, it's also a time to acquire the skills needed for jobs in the "real world," but the part about becoming an adult with ideals and integrity is also important.

MOYERS: Richard Hofstadter referred in particular to what he called "the national disrespect for mind" that he said characterized the country in the 1950s. Is that true of what's happening today or is this more a deliberate political strategy to try to put the opposition off balance? Do they disrespect the mind or are they in need of a political tool to weaponize the culture wars?

SCOTT: I think it's both. I think there is a disrespect for the mind that Trump, for example, exemplifies. His is a kind of strategic thinking that's more about shrewdness than about intellect. His attack on "elites" is meant to rally his base to rebel against the powers that be—in Washington especially. I don't think he cares much about higher education per se; he just wants to demonstrate that learning isn't necessary for business or government. He wants to elevate mediocrity to a heroic virtue. But I also think there's a concerted effort on the part of groups of the Bradley Foundation and the Koch brothers, of people like Betsy DeVos, to call into question the very function of public education in general and of the university in particular.

MOYERS: Back in the 1950s, when Sen. Joseph McCarthy (R-WI) railed against universities, artists, writers and journalists, his followers howled along with him in trying to persecute their perceived enemies. As you listen to what's happening today, do you ever hear McCarthy's voice resonating in your head?

SCOTT: I do. In some ways it's even worse today. The internet has made possible a frightening practice of threats and intimidation—threats of unspeakable violence and death. McCarthy was scary, but not like that. There's been a lot of talk about Left student groups violating the free speech of the Right. And certainly there are examples of students shouting down speakers whose political views they don't want to hear, views they think don't belong on a university campus. I certainly don't support that kind of behavior. But what's not been covered to the same extent is the attack by the Right on people with whom they disagree. A large number of university teachers have been targeted for speeches that they've made, they've been harassed and threatened. Take the case of Princeton's

Keeanga-Yamahtta Taylor. She gave a commencement speech at Hampshire College in which she called Trump a racist and a white supremacist. Fox News carried it, and she received hateful emails, among them death threats—she's African American—so there were threats to lynch her too. She canceled all of her speaking engagements because the threats were so violent. They make McCarthy look tame in comparison. McCarthy's were violent threats at a more abstract level. These are specific threats: "I have a gun pointed at your head." So there's something now about the unleashing of violent hateful speech that is more prevalent than it was even in the days of Joseph McCarthy.

MOYERS: If I may raise your personal story: Your father was suspended back then from his job as a high school social studies teacher and two years later he was fired because he refused to collaborate with an investigation into a purported communist infiltration in the New York public schools. How old were you at the time?

SCOTT: I was 10.

MOYERS: Were you afraid?

SCOTT: Yep. Although we weren't supposed to be afraid; we were supposed to be proud. And I certainly was proud of the principled stand he had taken. But yes, I was also afraid. FBI agents routinely came knocking at the door. The phone was certainly tapped. Years later I got a copy of my father's FBI file, most of which was redacted. There were all sorts of amazing things in it; things that I thought at the time were maybe paranoid worries on the part of my parents turned out to be even more true than I thought they were. A couple of times I gave the wrong birthdate to get a summer job before I was 18. They had my name in my father's FBI file with three different birthdays listed under it.

MOYERS: Father and daughter!

SCOTT: They were doing even that? I was 16, 17 years old. So we were certainly afraid. We were worried. I had friends whose fathers were in jail. But the personal danger was the fear of going to jail or losing one's job. The visceral expressions of hatred, the death threats, that are coming out now in social media. These are more frightening than my experiences as a kid.

MOYERS: How long was your father out of work?

SCOTT: He never taught again. He had different kinds of jobs doing educational projects or working in various other places. But he defined himself as a teacher and he lost that permanently.

MOYERS: What was your father's name?

SCOTT: Samuel Wallach.

MOYERS: His defense was both brave and eloquent. Let me read it to you:

> I've been a teacher for 15 years, a proud American teacher. I have tried all these years to inspire my youngsters with a deep devotion for the American way of life, our Constitution and Bill of Rights. Hundreds of my youngsters fought in World War II and I know their understanding of the need to fight for their country was inspired by my teaching and the Bill of Rights. . . . From that teaching, our youngsters got the feeling that we are living in a country where nobody has a right to ask what are your beliefs, how do you worship God, what you read.

"As a teacher and a believer in those fundamental principles, it seems to me," your father said, "that it would be a betrayal of everything I have been teaching to cooperate with the committee in an investigation of a man's opinions, political beliefs and private views." If I may say, that's one for the ages.

SCOTT: Yes it is.

MOYERS: Did he live long enough to see your career as a scholar unfold?

SCOTT: Yes. He lived until he was 91 and he was proud of me. He would be even prouder now, I think, of the kinds of things I've been saying lately about academic freedom. All of my work in some way or another speaks to political issues according to the upbringing that I had, which was deeply rooted in exactly those principles that you just read.

MOYERS: Ariel Dorfman has an essay in the current edition of *The New York Review of Books*. He says, "Never has an occupant of the White House exhibited such a toxic mix of ignorance and mendacity, such lack of intellectual curiosity and disregard for rigorous analysis." He describes what's happening as "an assault on national discourse, scientific knowledge and objective truth." Where is this taking us?

SCOTT: Oh God, where is this taking us? I hope not down the road of the kind of fascist thinking that was going on in Italy and Germany in the '20s and '30s, but it certainly feels we could move in that direction, toward an extremely dangerous authoritarian populism. Because the thing about education— and why I'm so passionate about the position and status of the university—is that it's supposed to teach citizens how to think better, how to think critically, how to tell truth from falsehood, how to make a judgment about when they're being lied to and duped and when they're not, how to evaluate scientific teaching. Losing that training of citizens is an extremely dangerous road to go down because it does open people to the kind of toxic influences that Dorfman describes.

MOYERS: Here's the challenge: Two-thirds of Americans today don't have college degrees. As politics last year and this year reveal, many of them have a deep resentment toward those who do, and toward the colleges and institutions that produce many of today's so-called elite. How do you persuade those people that academic freedom is relevant to their lives?

SCOTT: One way is that even before college and university, teaching in public schools K–12 has to deal with what it means to learn the truth; it has to teach respect for science, for the authority and lessons of history. It also has to teach kids to question things—how to question them. I think if you start this at a lower level than at university, people who didn't go to university would have some sense of how to make a judgment about the honesty or not of politicians. I think the anger that is being directed to universities and so-called elites at universities is actually an anger that's displaced from politicians (who promise to make things better and never do), from employers, it's an anger at the economic system that has put so many of these people out of the kind of work that once was so satisfying to them.

MOYERS: In your lectures and essays you use a term that we don't hear very often today. You say the pursuit of knowledge is not an elitist activity but a practice vital to democracy and to the promotion of the common good. What do you mean by the common good and how does academic freedom contribute to it?

SCOTT: What I mean by the common good is that we understand we're all part of something bigger than ourselves, that we live in societies together and must help take care of one another because you never know when you're going to need to be taken care of by others. And it's not enough to say that your family or your church is going to take care of you. Societies are collective entities, we're meant to be connected to one another; the function of government is to administer that connection. We've increasingly lost that sense of community, of the notion that there is something we contribute to and benefit from that is called the common good. I think I would date the beginnings of that loss to the Reagan administration and to the notion that somehow we were all separate individuals who only ought to be interested in ourselves. There were a number of court cases in the early '80s when class-action suits were brought, only to be thrown out by Reagan judges on the grounds that individual injury had to be proven, that you couldn't use statistics about discrimination in the labor force. You had to have individual cases and each one had to be remedied as an individual matter. There was the tax reform movement that treated progressive income taxes as assaults on individual autonomy rather than what they are—a shared responsibility for ourselves and others in the society that we all live in. People began to say they didn't want to pay property taxes any longer because they had no children in schools (and most property taxes were used to support the public schools). As if the education of society's children didn't have an impact even on childless people! The common good is the notion of shared collective responsibility and reciprocity. It's that that we've lost.

MOYERS: I grew up in a small town in East Texas in the '30s and '40s; I was the son of one of the poorest men in town but I was friends with the daughter of the richest man in town. Both of us went to good public elementary schools, shared the same good public library, played in the same good public park, drove down good public roads, attended the same good public high school, and eventually went on to good public colleges—all made possible by people who came before us, whom we would never know: Taxpayers!

SCOTT: They were people who were taking their responsibility for you in the sense that you were the next generation of a society that had benefited them and that they needed to benefit by continuing to support it.

MOYERS: You mentioned Ronald Reagan. His kindred spirit, Margaret Thatcher (prime minister of the United Kingdom), declared there is no such thing as society.

SCOTT: Yes. The late '70s and '80s—that's the beginning of the turn away from collective responsibility to a kind of selfish individualism that we now associate with or call neoliberalism.

MOYERS: So colleges and universities contribute to understanding the need for a social contract—pursuing knowledge and understanding is important to responsibility and reciprocity. You've said that there is an important distinction between the First Amendment right of free speech that we all enjoy in some circumstances and the principle of academic freedom that refers to teachers and the knowledge they produce and convey. What exactly is that distinction?

SCOTT: Well, free speech is what we all have and is guaranteed by the First Amendment of the U.S. Constitution. Academic freedom refers to what happens in the university, particularly in the classroom, and to the importance of the teacher having the right to teach and share what he or she has learned, has proven her competence to teach, having gone through a series of tests and certifications including research and writing to demonstrate her abilities and knowledge. I don't think students have academic freedom in that sense, but they do have the right of free speech; they can express themselves, but their ideas are not subject to the tests of the judgment of their peers or to scientific affirmation as teachers are. A biology teacher does not have to accept a student's essay that insists creationism rather than evolution is the explanation of how we got to be where we are. That student is not being denied his right of free speech when he's given a low grade for not having learned the biology. So the university is the place where the pursuit of truth is taught, the rules for learning how to pursue it are explained, and students begin to understand how to evaluate the seriousness of truth. Those are incredibly important lessons, and only the teachers' academic freedom can protect them because there will always be people who disagree with or disapprove of the ideas they are trying to convey. There are students whose religious upbringing is going to make them feel really uncomfortable in a class where certain kinds of secular ideas are being presented. There are students whose ideas about history or sexuality are going to be similarly challenged to question, to affirm, or to change those ideas. That doesn't mean that they shouldn't be exposed to them; that's why they're at school. That's why they come to school and to university: to be taught how to think well and critically about material that they're being presented with. But it's the teacher who is certified to teach them how to do that.

MOYERS: You write that free speech makes no distinction about quality; academic freedom does.

SCOTT: Yes, and there's actually a wonderful quote from Stanley Fish, who is sometimes very polemical and with whom I don't always agree. He writes, "Freedom of speech is not an academic value. Accuracy of speech is an academic value; completeness of speech is an academic value; relevance of speech is an academic value. Each of these is directly related to the goal of academic inquiry: getting a matter of fact right." Freedom of speech is not about that. Freedom of speech is about expressing your opinion, however bad or good, however right or wrong, and being able to defend it and argue it and be argued with about it in public forums. But that's not what academic freedom is about. That's not what the classroom is about. I would have a hard time banning even Richard Spencer [founder of the white nationalist movement] from speaking on a university campus, however hateful and dangerous I find his ideas.

MOYERS: You quote Robert Post, the former dean of Yale Law School, who seems to suggest that professors do not have an unfettered right of free speech in the classroom, that they're constrained by the need to teach their subject matter so that their job as educators limits their rights of free speech. Is he splitting hairs there?

SCOTT: Yes and no. I think he's right that the criticism of too much political advocacy in a physics class for example is something that one could reasonably object to, that students who come to learn math or physics and who have to hear a speech about the war in Iraq, for example, probably are right that they shouldn't have to, that that's not what they're there in that class for. It doesn't mean that that professor can't speak outside of the classroom on those issues. But where it gets tricky is in classes where, say, history classes and a professor is teaching material that some students find objectionable because they think it's too critical of the story that they want to be told.

MOYERS: In one of your lectures you asked some questions that were rhetorical in nature—

SCOTT: I asked, but didn't answer them—yes. Am I going to have to answer them now?

MOYERS: Yes, the reckoning is here. So—should a professor be able to teach that human activity does not contribute to global warming?

SCOTT: I think it's questionable. I'm with the climate scientists; I find it very hard to think that that would be a credible scientific position. How much human activity has contributed, OK, what other sorts of influences there have been, OK, but I think somebody getting up and saying that there is no proof whatsoever of human influence on climate change, I would have a hard time accepting the seriousness of a professor who taught that.

MOYERS: What's the difference between a climate denier and a Holocaust denier?

SCOTT: I think not much these days. I think not much at all because the climate denier tries to prove, as the Holocaust denier does, that the facts that demonstrate that there was a Holocaust and that there is climate change are wrong and don't exist—against all evidence that they exist.

MOYERS: Should a professor be able to teach creationism in the biology curriculum if half the students believe it?

SCOTT: No. Absolutely not.

MOYERS: Why?

SCOTT: Because, again, we're talking about what counts as science. If the students don't want to learn about evolution, they shouldn't be in the course. A biology course that teaches creationism is not a science course, it's a religion course. So the students demanding that creationism be given credence in that course are out of line and are denying the academic freedom of the professor. They are calling into question the scientific basis of the material that's being presented. And students are not in a position to do that.

MOYERS: So you're saying that both sides of that argument don't carry equal weight in the training of future scientists, right?

SCOTT: Yes, exactly.

MOYERS: Is there really no difference between the structures of discrimination experienced by African Americans and criticism of those structures leveled against whites?

SCOTT: I think there is a huge difference between those things because I think what is being pointed out by African Americans is that from slavery forward they have been living in a supposed democracy which treats them as less than other citizens, less than whites in the society. And I think that pointing out that there are structures of discrimination in the society, deeply rooted racist structures, that segregate housing, that send black children to ill-equipped schools, that discriminate in the workplace—these are truths about our society that must be faced. I don't know if you've seen Ta-Nehisi Coates's article in *The Atlantic*?

MOYERS: Yes I have.

SCOTT: Your question, or my own question, made me think about it. He makes a very passionate argument about the structures of racism that go deep in American society and that if we're going to correct them, must be addressed and pointed out, which is not to say that every white is a racist but that the way things are organized and the often unconscious biases that people bring to relations with African Americans, need to be put on the table and examined for what they are.

MOYERS: It makes a difference in lineage whether your great-grandfather owned slaves or was owned as a slave. Whether your grandfather was lynched or wore a white robe and did the lynching. Your circumstances can sometimes be traced back to those differences.

SCOTT: Yes—although probably not directly. But the structures that created those differences and those affiliations continue to organize life in our society.

MOYERS: Do you think that the strategy on the Right is to provoke situations that can be used to demonstrate that it's the Left that is shutting down freedom of speech today?

SCOTT: I do, yes. I think that's what people like Milo Yiannopoulos, the conservative provocateur, are all about. He comes to a campus, he insults people, he engages in the worst forms of racist and sexist speech. And the point is to provoke leftist reaction to him that can then be used to discredit the Left. And my sense is that what the Left needs to do is find strategies that will defuse the situation rather than play into their hands.

MOYERS: After the outbursts that greeted Yiannopoulos at the University of California at Berkeley, a city councilwoman there said, "I don't appreciate that these are racists coming to UC Berkeley to spew hate." Would you argue that racists should be silenced?

SCOTT: I don't think we can argue that. I think what we need to do is expose them for what they are and fight back. I think we need to let them speak. They have free speech rights. At the same time we have to argue that other groups must not be shut down, either—say, students standing up for Palestinian rights. They have the right to speak just as often and just as much as racists like Yiannopoulos or Richard Spencer. There has to be equal treatment of these groups even though the right-wing groups are, because of their publicity stunts, gathering all of the attention while quietly left-wing groups such as the Palestinian students are being shut down or—

MOYERS: You're not at peace with some of the behavior on the other side, either.

SCOTT: No.

MOYERS: You've warned about the moralism that's appeared in some college courses. And I know you have expressed some concern about so-called trigger warnings.

SCOTT: Well I think trigger warnings assume that students are fragile and need to be protected from difficult ideas. I don't think students need to be protected from difficult ideas. And I think the problem of trigger warnings is that they have been used to police what's taught in classes, to avoid subjects such as rape, violence, race—these need to be discussed.

MOYERS: What about minority students who have experienced considerable hostility growing up in an inhospitable culture, who have been silenced or marginalized by that hostility, and want colleges to be safe spaces against the hostile culture?

SCOTT: I don't think colleges are safe spaces. It's one thing to have a fraternity house or a community center where students can go and talk about their shared experiences. But it's another thing to have safe spaces in the sense that the university's providing them with protection from what they have to experience and find ways of protesting and resisting.

MOYERS: Let's talk about what happened at Middlebury College back in March. Charles Murray, the controversial author of *The Bell Curve*, a book some critics denounced as racist, was invited to speak at this small liberal arts college. Much of the audience turned their backs on him and a couple of hundred students chanted, "Black lives matter! Black lives matter!" and "Your message is hatred, we will not tolerate it." Murray finally had to deliver his talk via a video feed from a locked room. Ironically, perhaps, later reports suggested that the audience was driven less by Murray's work and by free speech rights than by the larger political forces of partisanship and polarization and anger throughout the country. Murray himself said that he and his audience probably had something in common: They all hated Trump. As you know, the Harvard scholar Danielle Allen took a position that angered some of her liberal friends. She compared Charles Murray's experience at Middlebury with that of the black high school students who integrated Central High School in Arkansas fifty years ago. They had to be protected by the National Guard from a violent white racist mob. Danielle Allen said that Charles Murray and his sponsors were like those students who were trying simply "to go to school." They were also "trying, simply, to keep school open. And in this moment they, too, were heroes." Were they?

SCOTT: I think the comparison is a bad one. Because in the one case, Little Rock, these kids were not just trying to keep school open, they were trying to integrate the school. An all-white school. They were trying to go to school in a school that had historically kept them out. So this was a protest against a longstanding form of discrimination that required enormous courage and resulted in fact in the integration of the school. To compare that to students protesting a speech by an invited outside speaker who has had no experience of that kind of discrimination, a white man, an academic who has always held a university position and despite the criticism of some of his work has never been removed from the tenured position that he enjoys—with all the privileges of an academic life—to compare that momentary experience of being shouted down or treated unfairly as he was (because I don't think they should have shouted him down)—it's just a comparison that makes no sense to me. It raises the incident with Charles Murray to a level that is not at all comparable or in the same register as the experience of the Little Rock Nine.

MOYERS: Earlier we both seemed to agree that there was a political motive to the Right's current attacks on the academy—and that what's involved is Trump's crusade to discredit his critics and opponents—as well as the Right's appetite for alternative facts to challenge knowledge-based and evidence-driven reality, which get in the way of their drive for power.

So there's a politically conservative outfit named the National Association of Scholars that wants to "evaluate the academic elite." They would eliminate peer review—that is, scholars charged to judge competence of professors and replace them with "experts" who are "of genuinely independent minds." They don't want you scholars assessing each other's work, they want someone on their side doing that. How does this play into the Right's attack on the academy and Trump's crusade against knowledge?

SCOTT: I think the National Association of Scholars is the inside group that's looking to transform the academy in conjunction with the outside group. I don't think they are probably coordinating with one another or maybe they are, but I think the effect is the same. Bringing in so-called neutral outside experts to judge the quality of academic work seems to be impossible because it's precisely within disciplines that the judgment and evaluation and regulation of academic work happens. If you're not in the discipline, you have no way of knowing what the standards are, what the history of changing modes of interpretation have been, whether the work is following acceptable patterns of proof and evidence. It just doesn't make any sense at all. Who are these "neutral outside experts?" What is the standard of neutrality that they're offering? Somebody who doesn't know anything about history and therefore can decide that our book about slavery is well done or not? Somebody who isn't a scientist or who is a scientist but is not trained to understand how physics operate and whether string theory is a good thing or a bad thing. What constitutes neutrality on the part of these so-called experts which is better than the expert judgment of peers—people within the discipline who understand how and why scholars do the research that they do?

MOYERS: So sum up the state of academic freedom in late 2017 as we approach the end of Trump's first full year in power.

SCOTT: It's under grave threat. And it's under grave threat from many different directions. And it's up to those of us in the academy who care about the universities and who love the teaching that we do, to somehow keep open that space of critical thinking and the pursuit of knowledge and the search for truth—to keep that space open and protected from the forces that would destroy it.

MOYERS: Thank you, Joan Scott.

NOTES

INTRODUCTION

I am grateful to Peter Coviello for his criticisms and suggestions.

1. Ellen Schrecker, *No Ivory Tower: McCarthyism and the Universities* (Oxford: Oxford University Press, 1986); and Marjorie Heins, *Priests of Our Democracy: The Supreme Court, Academic Freedom, and the Anti-Communist Purges* (New York: New York University Press, 2013).

2. Louis Menand, ed., *The Future of Academic Freedom* (Chicago: University of Chicago Press, 1996). See also Michael Bérubé and Cary Nelson, eds., *Higher Education Under Fire: Politics, Economics, and the Crisis of the Humanities* (New York: Routledge, 1995).

3. Diane Ravitch, "The Controversy over the National History Standards," *Bulletin of the American Academy of Arts and Sciences* 51, no. 3 (January–February 1998): 14–28, doi:10.2307/3824089; and Gary B. Nash, Charlotte Antoinette Crabtree, and Ross E. Dunn, *History on Trial: Culture Wars and the Teaching of the Past* (New York: Knopf, 1997).

4. Jane Mayer, "A Conservative Nonprofit that Seeks to Transform College Campuses Faces Allegations of Racial Bias and Illegal Campaign Activity," *New Yorker*, December 21, 2017.

5. John Higgins, "Abstract Human Right or Material Practice? Academic Freedom in an Unequal Society," in *State of the Nation: Poverty and Inequality: Diagnosis, Prognosis and Responses*, ed. Crain Soudien, Ingrid Woolard, and Vasu Reddy (Cape Town, SA: Human Sciences Research Council Press, 2018). See also John Higgins, *Academic Freedom in a*

Democratic South Africa: Essays and Interviews on Higher Education and the Humanities (Lewisburg, PA: Bucknell University Press, 2014).

6. Menand, *The Future of Academic Freedom*, 4.

7. Adam Sitze, "Academic Unfreedom, Unacademic Freedom," *Massachusetts Review* 58, no. 4 (Winter 2017): 597.

8. Sitze, "Academic Unfreedom," 599. In this connection, Sitze points to the limits of the marketplace metaphor: "The more this doctrine monopolizes our thinking, the more it fails on its own terms, all while also authoring a profound academic irresponsibility in its adherents: rather than ask what our responsibility for what academic discourse can or should be, we simply let the market decide instead. The truth of the doctrine of the marketplace of ideas is that it excludes any truth except the laws of the marketplace itself." Sitze, "Academic Unfreedom," 597.

9. University of Wisconsin–Madison KnowledgeBase, "Sifting and Winnowing," n.d., https://kb.wisc.edu/page.php?id=10452.

10. Matthew W. Finkin and Robert C. Post, *For the Common Good: Principles of American Academic Freedom* (New Haven, Conn.: Yale University Press, 2009), 42.

11. Finkin and Post, *For the Common Good*, 39.

12. "1940 Statement of Principles on Academic Freedom and Tenure with 1970 Interpretive Comments," available at AAUP.org, https://www.aaup.org/file/1940%20Statement.pdf.

13. Bill Readings, *The University in Ruins* (Cambridge, Mass.: Harvard University Press, 1996); and Christopher Newfield, *The Great Mistake: How We Wrecked Public Universities and How We Can Fix Them* (Baltimore, Md.: Johns Hopkins University Press, 2016).

14. Scott Carlson, "When College Was a Public Good," *Chronicle of Higher Education*, November 27, 2016, https://www.chronicle.com/article/When-College-Was-a-Public-Good/238501. See also Michael Fabricant and Stephen Brier, *Austerity Blues: Fighting for the Soul of Public Higher Education* (Baltimore, Md.: Johns Hopkins University Press, 2016); and Denise Cummins, "Think Tenure Protects You? with Wealthy Donors and Less Public Funding, Think Again," *PBS Newshour*, October 1, 2014. http://www.pbs.org/newshour/naking-sense/think-tenure-protects.

15. Wendy Brown, *Undoing the Demos: Neoliberalism's Stealth Revolution* (Brooklyn, N.Y.: Zone Books, 2015), 178.

16. Brown, *Undoing the Demos*, 39.

17. Carlson, "When College Was a Public Good."

18. Judith Butler, "Limits on Free Speech?" *Academe Blog* December 7, 2017, https://academeblog.org/2017/12/07/free-expression-or-harassment/.

19. Finkin and Post, *For the Common Good*, 44.

20. An example is *Public Research Universities: Serving the Public Good* (Cambridge, Mass.: American Academy of Arts and Sciences, 2016), https://www.amacad.org/multimedia/pdfs/publications/researchpapersmonographs/PublicResearchUniv_PublicGood.pdf.

21. See, for example, "2018–22 Strategic Plan: Educating for Democracy," American Association of Colleges and Universities, https://www.aacu.org/about/strategicplan. See also Robert B. Reich, *The Common Good* (New York: Knopf, 2018).

22. Higgins, "Abstract Human Right."

23. Jonathan Cole, "Academic Freedom Under Fire," in *Who's Afraid of Academic Freedom?*, ed. Akeel Bilgrami and Jonathan R. Cole (New York: Columbia University Press, 2015), 51.

24. Edward Said, "Identity, Authority, and Freedom," in *The Future of Academic Freedom*, ed. Louis Menand (Chicago: University of Chicago Press, 1996), 223.

25. John Dewey, "Academic Freedom," in *John Dewey. The Middle Works: 1899–1924*, ed. Jo Ann Boydston (Carbondale: Southern Illinois University Press, 1976), 62–63.

1. ACADEMIC FREEDOM AS
AN ETHICAL PRACTICE

This essay was first published in Louis Menand, ed. *The Future of Academic Freedom* (Chicago: University of Chicago Press, 1996). I wish to thank Wendy Brown, Judith Butler, Stefan Collini, Christopher Fynsk, Peter Galison, Tony Scott, and the members of the Twentieth Century Seminar at the CUNY Graduate Center for their critical suggestions.

1. Fritz Machlup, "On Some Misconceptions Concerning Academic Freedom" (1955), in *Academic Freedom and Tenure: A Handbook of the*

148 ⁞ I. ACADEMIC FREEDOM AS AN ETHICAL PRACTICE

American Association of University Professors, ed. Louis Joughin (Madison: University of Wisconsin Press, 1967), 192.

2. Michel de Certeau, "History: Science and Fiction," in *Heterologies: Discourse on the Other*, trans. Brian Massumi (Minneapolis: University of Minnesota Press, 1986), 199.

3. Wendy Brown, Introduction to *States of Injury: Studies in Power and Freedom in Late Modernity* (Princeton, N.J.: Princeton University Press, 1995), 6.

4. See de Certeau, "History: Science and Fiction," 199.

5. William Haver, "Apres moi le Deleuze: The Question of Practice" (unpublished paper, 1992), 29.

6. John Dewey, "Academic Freedom," in *John Dewey: The Middle Works, 1899–1924*, vol. 2, *Essays on Logical Theory, 1902–1903*, ed. Jo Ann Boydston (Carbondale: Southern Illinois University Press, 1976), 56.

7. Dewey, "Academic Freedom," 58.

8. Dewey, "Academic Freedom," 56–58.

9. Dewey, "Academic Freedom," 64.

10. Dewey, "Academic Freedom," 64.

11. Dewey, "Academic Freedom," 59.

12. Dewey, "Academic Freedom," 60.

13. Dewey, "Academic Freedom," 65–66.

14. Dewey, "Academic Freedom," 66.

15. Arthur O. Lovejoy, "Academic Freedom," *Encyclopedia of the Social Sciences*, ed. E. R. A. Seligman (New York: Macmillan, 1937), 1:384.

16. Glenn Morrow, "Academic Freedom" in *International Encyclopedia of the Social Sciences*, ed. David L. Sills (New York: Macmillan and Free Press, 1968), 1:5–6.

17. On the question of "relevance," see Jesse Lemisch, "Radical Scholarship as Scientific Method and Anti-Authoritarianism, Not 'Relevance,'" *New University Conference Papers* 2 (1970). See also the discussion of the debates in this period in Peter Novick, *That Noble Dream: The "Objectivity Question" and the American Historical Profession* (New York: Cambridge University Press, 1988), 415–68. See also Bruce Robbins, *Secular Vocations: Intellectuals, Professionalism, Culture* (London: Verso, 1993), esp. 80–83.

18. On the erotic component of pedagogy, see Jane Gallop, "Sex and Sexism: Feminism and Harassment Policy," *Academe* 80 (September/October 1994): 16–23.

19. Wendy Brown, "Toward a Genealogy of Contemporary Political Moralism," in *Democracy, Community, Citizenship*, ed. Tom Keenan and Kendall Thomas (London: Verso, 1995).

20. For examples of this kind of "postmodernist" bashing, see Joyce Appleby, Lynn Hunt, and Margaret Jacob, *Telling the Truth about History* (New York: Norton, 1994); and Paul R. Gross and Norman Levitt, *Higher Superstition: The Academic Left and Its Quarrels with Science* (Baltimore: Johns Hopkins University Press, 1994).

21. On this, see "Who Stole Feminism? How Women Have Betrayed Women," by Christina Holf Sommers, a special issue of *Democratic Culture* (the newsletter of Teachers for a Democratic Culture), vol. 3, no. 2 (Fall 1994), https://files.eric.ed.gov/fulltext/ED377780.pdf. In this special symposium edition of *Democratic Culture*, the articles by Nina Auerbach, "Christina's World," and Rebecca Sinkler, "The Choice of Nina Auerbach," detail the episode about the book review.

22. Katherine J. Mayberry, "White Feminists Who Study Black Writers," *Chronicle of Higher Education*, October 12, 1994, A48.

23. See Haver, "Apres moi le Deleuze," 2.

24. See Novick, *That Noble Dream*, chap. 16.

25. I want to point out here that not all critics of disciplinarity are political instrumentalists or fundamentalists.

26. For a compelling analysis of this issue, see John Guillory, *Cultural Capital: The Problem of Literary Canon Formation* (Chicago: University of Chicago Press, 1993).

27. Thanks to Tony Scott for his help with these formulations. On the question of community, see Jean-Luc Nancy, *The Inoperative Community* (Minneapolis: University of Minnesota Press, 1991); and Miami Theory Collective, ed., *Community at Loose Ends* (Minneapolis: University of Minnesota Press, 1991), esp. the article by Christopher Fynsk, "Community and the Limits of Theory," 19–29.

28. On understanding as the goal of humanistic scholarship, see Stefan Collini, "Research in the Humanities," *TLS*, April 3, 1987, 349–50.

29. "Response to an Inquiry by Professor Paul Brest," in "Report of Committee A for 1985–86," *Academe* 72 (September 1986): 13a, 19a; cited in *Academe* 74 (September–October 1988): 55.

30. On the loss of the teleological historical narrative, see Brown, "Toward a Genealogy."

2. KNOWLEDGE, POWER, AND ACADEMIC FREEDOM

This essay was first published in *Social Research* 76, no. 2 (Summer 2009): 451–80.

1. American Association of University Professors (AAUP), "General Report of the Committee on Academic Freedom and Academic Tenure," *Bulletin of the MUP* 1, no. 1 (December 1915): 20–43.

2. John Dewey. "Academic Freedom," *John Dewey: The Middle Works: 1899–1942*, vol. 2, *Essays on Logical Theory, 1902–1903*, ed. Jo Ann Boydston (Carbondale: Southern Illinois University Press, 1976), 62–63.

3. Frank Donoghue, *The Last Professors: The Corporate University and the Fate of the Humanities* (New York: Fordham University Press, 2008), 1–23.

4. AAUP, "General Report," 32.

5. AAUP, "General Report," 36.

6. Dewey, "Academic Freedom," 58.

7. Dewey, "Academic Freedom," 57.

8. Michel de Certeau, "History: Science and Fiction," in *Heterologies: Discourse on the Other*, trans. Brian Massumi (Minneapolis: University of Minnesota Press, 1986).

9. Walter Metzger, "The Age of the University," in *The Development of Academic Freedom in the United States*, by Richard Hofstadter and Walter Metzger (New York: Columbia University Press, 1955), 438.

10. Metzger, "The Age of the University," 442–43.

11. "Report Concerning the University of Pennsylvania," *Bulletin of the AAUP* (1916), 132.

12. "Report Concerning the University of Pennsylvania," 135.

13. "Report Concerning the University of Pennsylvania," 138.

14. "Report Concerning the University of Pennsylvania," 139.

15. AAUP, "General Report," 27.

16. AAUP, "General Report," 22.

17. AAUP, "General Report," 23.

18. AAUP, "General Report," 32.

19. AAUP, "General Report," 24.

20. AAUP, "General Report," 28–29.

21. AAUP, "General Report," 28.

22. AAUP, "General Report," 34.

23. AAUP, "General Report," 35.

24. AAUP, "General Report," 28. Here the declaration reads like a conversation among the authors, with the majority conceding some points to more conservative colleagues while returning again and again to the main point: the need for absolute freedom in the classroom.

25. AAUP, "General Report," 34.

26. Ellen Schrecker, *No Ivory Tower: McCarthyism and the Universities* (New York: Oxford University Press, 1986), 198.

27. Arthur O. Lovejoy, "Academic Freedom," *Encyclopedia of the Social Sciences*, vol. 1, ed. E. R. A. Seligman (New York: Macmillan, 1937), 384; and Glenn Morrow, "Academic Freedom," *International Encyclopedia of the Social Sciences*, vol. 1, ed. David L. Sills (New York: Macmillan and the Free Press, 1968), 5–6.

28. Norman Hampson, "The Big Store," *London Review of Books* 4, no. 1 (January 21, 1987): 17–18; and Lawrence Stone, "Only Women," *New York Review of Books*, April 11, 1985, 21–27.

29. John Searle, "Rationality and Realism: What Is at Stake?" *Daedalus* 122 (Fall 1992): 72.

30. "Response to an Inquiry by Professor Paul Brest," in "Report of Committee A for 1985–86." *Academe* 72 (September 1986): 13a, 19a. Cited again in *Academe 74* (September–October 1988): 55.

31. AAUP, "General Report," 33.

32. AAUP, "General Report," 33.

33. Dewey, "Academic Freedom," 59.

34. AAUP, "General Report," 37.

35. Dewey, "Academic Freedom," 60.

36. "Report Concerning the University of Pennsylvania," 146.

37. "Report Concerning the University of Pennsylvania," 146.

38. "1940 Statement of Principles on Academic Freedom and Tenure," *Policy Documents and Reports*, 9th ed. (2001): 3–10.

39. AAUP, "General Report," 37.
40. "1940 Statement of Principles," 36.
41. "Academic Freedom and Tenure: The University of Illinois," *AAUP Bulletin*, Spring 1963, 26.
42. "Academic Freedom and Tenure," 27.
43. "Academic Freedom and Tenure," 28.
44. "Academic Freedom and Tenure," 34.
45. "Academic Freedom and Tenure," 37.
46. "Academic Freedom and Tenure," 40.
47. "Academic Freedom and Tenure," 41.
48. "Academic Freedom and Tenure," 42.
49. "Academic Freedom and Tenure," 43.
50. "Academic Freedom and Tenure," 43.
51. Christopher Lasch, *The Agony of the American Left* (New York: Knopf, 1969), 83.
52. "Reports on Academic Freedom and Tenure: The University of California at Los Angeles," *AAUP Bulletin*, Autumn 1971, 398.
53. Note that this took place before Davis was indicted in the jailbreak attempt of George Jackson. "Reports on Academic Freedom and Tenure," 391.
54. "Reports on Academic Freedom and Tenure," 417.
55. "A Statement of the Association's Council: Freedom and Responsibility" (1970), *Policy Documents and Reports*, 9th ed. (2001): 136.
56. Stanley Fish, *Save the World on Your Own Time* (Oxford: Oxford University Press, 2008).
57. Arizona State Legislature, Senate proposed legislation, Spring 2008.

3. CIVILITY, AFFECT, AND ACADEMIC FREEDOM

This paper was presented at a conference on academic freedom at the University of Michigan, Ann Arbor, on October 8, 2015. A shortened and somewhat different version of it was published as "The New Thought Police," in *The Nation*, April 15, 2015. Thanks to Wendy Brown especially, and to Judith Butler, Brian Connolly, Hank Reichman, and Elizabeth Weed for helpful criticisms and suggestions.

1. AAUP, "Academic Freedom and Tenure: The University of Illinois at Urbana-Champaign," April 2015, https://www.aaup.org/report/UIUC.

2. Chancellor Wise's statement was found (but is no longer available) at http://illinois.edu/blog/view/1109/115906?count=1&ACTION =DIALOG&sort=aasc.

3. Hank Reichman, "Is 'Incivility' the New Communism?" *Academe Blog*, September 8, 2014, http://academeblog.org/2014/09/08/is-incivility -the-new-communism.

4. Quoted in Colleen Flaherty, "The Problem with Civility," *Inside Higher Ed*, September 9, 2014, https://www.insidehighered.com/news /2014/09/09/berkeley-chancellor-angers-faculty-members-remarks -civility-and-free-speech. Under intense criticism, some of which is reported in this article, Dirks modified these statements, distinguishing between civility and free speech.

5. Hank Reichman, "And Now There's a Blacklist?" *Academe Blog*, September 10, 2014, http://academeblog.org/2014/09/10/and-now-theres-a -blacklist.

6. "U.S. Jewish Group Accused of McCarthyism After Publishing List of Pro-Boycott Professors," *Haaretz*, September 16, 2014, http://www .haaretz.com/misc/haaretzcomsmartphoneapp/.premium-u-s-jewish -group-puts-out-blacklist-1.5301544. See also the AMCHA Initiative website, https://amchainitiative.org/.

7. Special Envoy to Monitor and Combat Anti-Semitism, "Defining Anti-Semitism," Fact Sheet, U.S. Department of State, June 8, 2010, https://2009-2017.state.gov/j/drl/rls/fs/2010/122352.htm.

8. Michelle Boorstein, "Arun Gandhi Quits Peace Institute in Flap Over Blog Posting," *Washington Post*, January 26, 2008, http://www .washingtonpost.com/wp-dyn/content/article/2008/01/25/AR2008012 502802.html.

9. David Bernstein, "Yale Episcopal Chaplain Rev. Bruce Shipman Digs Deeper," *Washington Post*, August 27, 2014, https://www.washingtonpost .com/news/volokh-conspiracy/wp/2014/08/27/yale-episcopal-chaplain -rev-bruce-shipman-digs-deeper/?utm_term=.401fa9f89369. See also the report in *Inside Higher Ed*, Flaherty, "The Problem with Civility."

10. Quoted in Flaherty, "The Problem with Civility."

11. Michael Meranze, "The Order of Civility," UC Santa Barbara Faculty Association, September 7, 2014, http://ucsbfa.org/the-order-of-civility/.

12. Jan Goldstein, Vicki Ruiz, and Kenneth Pomeranz, "Letter of Concern to University of Illinois Chancellor Regarding Salaita Case (2014),"

American Historical Association, August 31, 2014, https://www
.historians.org/news-and-advocacy/statements-and-resolutions-of
-support-and-protest/letter-of-concern-to-university-of-illinois
-chancellor-regarding-salaita-case.

13. Quoted in Norbert Elias, *The Civilizing Process: Sociogenetic and Psychogenetic Investigations* (Oxford: Blackwell, 2000), 34.

14. Elias, *The Civilizing Process*, 49.

15. Elias, *The Civilizing Process*, 34.

16. Elias, *The Civilizing Process*, 431.

17. Kathleen M. Brown, *Foul Bodies: Cleanliness in Early America* (New Haven, Conn.: Yale University Press, 2009), 9.

18. William Chafe, *Civilities and Civil Rights: Greensboro, North Carolina and the Black Struggle for Freedom* (Oxford: Oxford University Press, 1981).

19. John Murray Cuddihy, *The Ordeal of Civility: Freud, Marx, Levi-Strauss and the Jewish Struggle with Modernity* (Boston: Beacon, 1974).

20. Nancy Fraser, "Rethinking the Public Sphere: A Contribution to the Critique of Actually Existing Democracy," *Social Text*, no. 25–26 (1990): 56–80. See also, Nancy Fraser, "What's Critical About Critical Theory? The Case of Habermas and Gender," *New German Critique*, no. 335 (Spring–Summer 1985): 97–131.

21. *Inside Higher Ed*'s surveys are found at https://www.insidehighered.com/print/news/survey/.

22. "Civility, You, and Mizzou," University of Missouri website, n.d., https://understand.missouri.edu/civility-you-mizzou/.

23. The relevant slides from the conference are found at https://vdocuments.net/university-of-wisconsin-oshkosh-august-2011-academic-freedom-and-free-speech-require-open-safe-civil-and-collegial-campus-environments-grounded-in.html.

24. Cited in Ian Ward, "Democratic Civility and the Dangers of Niceness," *Political Theology* 18, no. 2 (2017): 115–36, http://www.tandfonline.com/doi/full/10.1080/1462317X.2016.1227047?src=recsys.

25. Quoted in Flaherty, "The Problem with Civility"; emphasis added. Another example of the association of civility with safety comes from a conference at the University of Wisconsin, Oshkosh in 2011. The conference report concluded that "Academic freedom and free speech

require open, safe, civil and collegial campus environments." http://slideplayer.com/slide/10771653/.

26. AMCHA Initiative website, https://amchainitiative.org/.

27. "UCSC Lecturer Tammi Benjamin Accuses Muslim and Palestinian Student Groups of Connections to Terror," YouTube, February 7, 2013, https://www.youtube.com/watch?v=UnSlbOhZgGI.

28. Lauren Gail Berlant, *Cruel Optimism* (Durham N.C.: Duke University Press, 2011).

29. Wendy Brown, *Undoing the Demos: Neoliberalism's Stealth Revolution* (Brooklyn N.Y.: Zone, 2015), 17.

30. I think there is a connection between the emphasis on affect in relation to campus speech and the turn to it by some scholars of history, literature, anthropology. It's no coincidence, I'm sure, that their attention to affect is part of a larger shift—one of those tectonic or archaeological shifts as Foucault identified them.

31. Chris Lorenz, "If You're so Smart, Why Are You Under Surveillance? Universities, Neoliberalism, and New Public Management," *Critical Inquiry* 38, no. 3 (Spring 2012): 621.

32. Michelle Goldberg, "This Professor Was Fired for Saying 'Fuck No' in Class," *Nation*, July 2, 2015.

33. The NCHERM Group, https://www.ncherm.org/.

34. Benno C. Schmidt, *Governance for a New Era: A Blueprint for Higher Education Trustees* (Washington, D.C.: American Council of Trustees and Alumni, August 2014).

35. This was language used in a Supreme Court decision in May 1999, *Davis v. Monroe County Board of Education.* It is also used in a number of legislative documents, including Title IX. "The Supreme Court; Excerpts from Decision on Sexual Harassment," *New York Times*, May 25, 1999, http://www.nytimes.com/1999/05/25/us/the-supreme-court-excerpts-from-decision-on-sexual-harassment.html.

36. Henry Louis Gates Jr., "Critical Race Theory and Freedom of Speech," in *The Future of Academic Freedom*, ed. Louis Menand (Chicago: University of Chicago Press, 1996), 149.

37. Weber Shandwick and Powell Tate, in partnership with KRC Research, conducts an annual nationwide survey titled "Civility in America." "We hope that our ongoing investigation of this critically important issue can help in at least a small way to restore civility in public life and bring

meaningful and long-lasting solutions to our ways of interacting and behaving in all aspects of American life. Incivility has become the default in too many of our interactions and it is affecting the very fabric of society." Note the disappearance of political differences as a problem—civility (or its negation) is somehow a new kind of behavior that has no context or cause. It is a cause unto itself. "Civility in America: An Annual Nationwide Survey," Weber Shandwick and Powell Tate, January 1, 2012, http://www.webershandwick.com/news/article/civility.

38. Judith Butler, *Excitable Speech: A Politics of the Performative* (New York: Routledge, 1997), 79–80.

39. Gates, "Critical Race Theory," 148.

40. Gates, "Critical Race Theory," 143.

41. AAUP, "Academic Freedom and Tenure." Chancellor Wise's statement is no longer available online (see note 2).

42. Peter Schmidt, "Campaigns Against Microaggressions Prompt Big Concerns About Free Speech," *Chronicle of Higher Education*, July 9, 2015, https://www.chronicle.com/article/Campaigns-Against/231459; and Derald Wing Sue, *Microaggressions in Everyday Life: Race, Gender, and Sexual Orientation* (Hoboken, N.J.: Wiley, 2010).

43. Butler, *Excitable Speech*, 50.

44. AAUP, "On Trigger Warnings," August 2014, https://www.aaup.org /report/trigger-warnings.

45. Jeannie Suk Gerson, "The Trouble with Teaching Rape Law," *New Yorker*, December 15, 2014, https://www.newyorker.com/news/news -desk/trouble-teaching-rape-law.

46. Gerson, "The Trouble with Teaching Rape Law."

47. Dave Huber, "Crafton Hills Reverses Course, Says 'No' to Course 'Trigger Warning' Notice," *College Fix*, July 15, 2015, https://www .thecollegefix.com/post/23349/.

48. AAUP, "On Trigger Warnings."

49. Joan Bertin, "Public Comment of Joan Bertin, to the US House of Representatives," June 11, 2015, 1, https://d28htnjz2elwuj.cloudfront.net/wp -content/uploads/2015/06/15104040/Public-Comment-of-Joan-Bertin -Executive-Director-National-Coalition-Against-Censorship.pdf. It is important to note that since I wrote this, Secretary of Education Betsy DeVos has appointed a committee to revise these recommendations. Some of her criticisms accord with those of the AAUP report; others

seem to want to weaken provisions of the legislation that address real problems of sexual harassment and assault on campus, especially those that take seriously victims' complaints.

50. AAUP, "The History, Uses and Abuses of Title IX," June 2016, https:// www.aaup.org/report/history-uses-and-abuses-title-ix.

51. Jeannie Suk Gersen, "Laura Kipnis's Endless Trial by Title IX," *New Yorker*, September 20, 2017, https://www.newyorker.com/news/news -desk/laura-kipniss-endless-trial-by-title-ix. See also Laura Kipnis, "Sexual Panic Strikes Academe," *Chronicle of Higher Education*, February 27, 2015.

52. Scott Jaschik, "Too Risky for Boulder?" *Inside Higher Ed*, December 16, 2013, https://www.insidehighered.com/news/2013/12/16/tenured -professor-boulder-says-she-being-forced-out-over-lecture-prosti tution.

53. Colleen Flaherty, "Fired for Being Profane," *Inside Higher Ed*, September 2, 2015, https://www.insidehighered.com/news/2015/09/02 /aaup-report-alleges-violations-academic-freedom-due-process-new -report-professors.

54. Colleen Flaherty, "Profanity, Not Pedagogy," *Inside Higher Ed*, January 15, 2018, https://www.insidehighered.com/news/2018/01/15/court -rejects-first-amendment-suit-professor-fired-over-her-use-profanity.

55. Bertin, "Public Comment," 1.

56. Brown, *Undoing the Demos*, 222.

4. ACADEMIC FREEDOM AND THE STATE

This was the keynote address for the conference on academic freedom at the Central European University in Budapest, June 22, 2017. The CEU was then under attack by the authoritarian government of the prime minister of Hungary, Viktor Orbán. At the time of publication of this book, its future was still uncertain.

1. Bill Readings, *The University in Ruins* (Cambridge, Mass.: Harvard University Press, 1996), 15. See also Richard Hofstadter and Walter P. Metzger, *The Development of Academic Freedom in the United States* (New York: Columbia University Press, 1955).

2. Immanuel Kant, *The Conflict of the Faculties*, trans. Mary J. Gregor (Lincoln: University of Nebraska Press, 1992).

3. Masao Miyoshi, "Ivory Tower in Escrow," *boundary 2* 27, no. 1 (Spring 2000): 11–12.

4. Miyoshi, "Ivory Tower in Escrow," 13.

5. Miyoshi, "Ivory Tower in Escrow," 13.

6. Edward Said, "Identity, Authority, and Freedom: The Potentate and the Traveler," in *The Future of Academic Freedom*, ed. Louis Menand (Chicago: University of Chicago Press, 1996), 218.

7. Said, "Identity, Authority, and Freedom," 219.

8. Said, "Identity, Authority, and Freedom," 220.

9. Said, "Identity, Authority, and Freedom," 220.

10. Said, "Identity, Authority, and Freedom," 223.

11. Said, "Identity, Authority, and Freedom," 223.

12. Said, "Identity, Authority, and Freedom," 223.

13. Said, "Identity, Authority, and Freedom," 227.

14. Said, "Identity, Authority, and Freedom," 227.

15. American Association of University Professors, "General Report of the Committee on Academic Freedom and Tenure," *Bulletin of the AAUP* 1, no. 1 (December 1915): 32. See also "Appendix I: 1915 Declaration of Principles on Academic Freedom and Academic Tenure," https://www.aaup.org/NR/rdonlyres/A6520A9D-0A9A-47B3-B550-C006B5B224E7/0/1915Declaration.pdf.

16. AAUP, "General Report," 36.

17. On the Ely case, see Hans-Joerg Tiede, *University Reform: The Founding of the American Association of University Professors* (Baltimore, Md.: Johns Hopkins University Press, 2015).

18. Theodore Herfurth, *Sifting and Winnowing: A Chapter in the History of Academic Freedom at the University of Wisconsin* (Madison: University of Wisconsin, 1949), http://www.library.wisc.edu/etext/WIReader/Contents/Sifting.html.

19. John Dewey, "Academic Freedom," in *John Dewey: The Middle Works, 1899–1924*, vol. 2, *Essays on Logical Theory, 1902–1903*, ed. Jo Ann Boydston (Carbondale: Southern Illinois University Press, 1976), 66.

20. Robert Post, "The Classic First Amendment Tradition Under Stress: Freedom of Speech and the University" in *The Free Speech Century*, ed. Lee C. Bollinger and Geoffrey R. Stone (Oxford: Oxford University Press, 2018). On these issues, see also Matthew W. Finkin and

Robert C. Post, *For the Common Good: Principles of American Academic Freedom* (New Haven, Conn.: Yale University Press, 2005).

21. Post, "The Classic First Amendment Tradition."

22. Said, "Identity, Authority, and Freedom," 223.

23. Nico Savidge, "Changes to Tenure, Budget and Regents Show Extent of Scott Walker's Impact on UW," *Wisconsin State Journal*, March 27, 2016, http://host.madison.com/wsj/news/local/education/university/changes -to-tenure-budget-and-regents-show-extent-of-scott/article_90954155 -df31-5fdb-bb93-dd93a0f81225.html; and Hans-Joerg Tiede, "Tenure and the University of Wisconsin System," AAUP website, May–June 2016, https://www.aaup.org/article/tenure-and-university-wiscon sin-system#.WqxF-IIh3BI.

24. Said, "Identity, Authority, and Freedom," 222.

25. Readings, *The University in Ruins*; and Christopher Newfield, *The Great Mistake: How We Wrecked Public Universities and How We Can Fix Them* (Baltimore, Md.: Johns Hopkins University Press, 2016). See also, Christopher Newfield, *Unmaking the Public University: The Forty-Year Assault on the Middle Class* (Cambridge, Mass.: Harvard University Press, 2008).

5. ON FREE SPEECH AND ACADEMIC FREEDOM

This essay was first given as a talk at the American Academy of Arts and Sciences when I was awarded the Talcott Parsons Prize for outstanding contributions to the social sciences, April 6, 2017.

1. *New York Times*, October 2, 1948.

2. Richard Hofstadter, *Anti-Intellectualism in American Life* (New York: Knopf, 1963), 3.

3. Hofstadter, *Anti-Intellectualism in American Life*, 6.

4. "Betsy DeVos' Entire CPAC Speech," *CNN*, February 24, 2017, http:// www.cnn.com/videos/politics/2017/02/23/cpac-betsy-devos-entire -remarks-sot.cnn.

5. The mission of Professor Watchlist is to expose and document college professors who discriminate against conservative students and advance so-called leftist propaganda in the classroom.

6. Sarah Lee, "Arizona Lawmaker Introduces Bill to Ban Taxpayer Funds for Social Justice Classes," *Blaze*, January 8, 2017, https://www.theblaze

.com/news/2017/01/08/arizona-lawmaker-introduces-bill-to-ban
-taxpayer-funds-for-social-justice-classes. See also Hank Reichman,
"Will Promoting 'Social Justice' Be Illegal in Arizona Universities?"
Academe Blog, January 14, 2017, https://academeblog.org/2017/01/14
/will-promoting-social-justice-be-illegal-in-arizona-universities/.

7. "Arkansas Legislator Pushes to Ban Books by historian Howard Zinn's
from Public Schools," *Project Censored*, April 6, 2017, http://project
censored.org/arkansas-legislator-pushes-ban-books-historian
-howard-zinns-public-schools/.

8. Colleen Flaherty, "Iowa Bill Would Force 'Partisan Balance' in Hiring," *Inside Higher Ed*, February 21, 2017, https://www.insidehighered
.com/quicktakes/2017/02/21/iowa-bill-would-force-partisan-balance
-hiring/.

9. Martin Kich, "The Answer to Campus Unrest—Another Kent State,"
Academe Blog, February 10, 2017, https://academeblog.org/2017/02/10
/the-answer-to-campus-unrest-another-kent-state/.

10. Tamara Best, "White Supremacists Step Up Recruiting on Campus
in Over 30 States, Report Says," *New York Times*, March 7, 2017.

11. Robert Post, "The Classic First Amendment Tradition Under Stress:
Freedom of Speech and the University" in *The Free Speech Century*, ed.
Lee C. Bollinger and Geoffrey R. Stone (Oxford: Oxford University
Press, 2018).

12. Post, "The Classic First Amendment Tradition."

13. Post, "The Classic First Amendment Tradition."

14. Post, "The Classic First Amendment Tradition."

15. Post, "The Classic First Amendment Tradition."

16. "Campus Free Speech: A Legislative Proposal," Goldwater Institute,
January 30, 2017, http://goldwaterinstitute.org/en/work/topics/consti
tutional-rights/free-speech/campus-free-speech-a-legislative-pro
posal/.

17. John K. Wilson, "The Tennessee Legislature's Attack on Free Speech,"
Academe Blog, February 12, 2017, https://academeblog.org/2017/02/12
/the-tennessee-legislatures-attack.

18. John K. Wilson, "The Dangerous NAS Proposals for the Higher Education Act," *Academe Blog*, February 23, 2017, https://academeblog.org
/2017/02/23/the-dangerous-nas-proposals-for-the-higher-education
-act/.

19. "Inside Every Liberal Is a Totalitarian Screaming to Get Out," May 21, 2013, https://www.frontpagemag.com/fpm/189984/inside-every-liberal -totalitarian-screaming-get-frontpagemagcom.

20. Danielle Allen, "Why Middlebury's Violent Response to Charles Murray Reminded Me of the Little Rock Nine," *Washington Post*, March 7, 2107.

21. Post, "The Classic First Amendment Tradition."

22. Robert P. George and Cornel West, "Sign the Statement: Truth Seeking, Democracy, and Freedom of Thought and Expression—A Statement by Robert P. George and Cornel West," Princeton University, James Madison Program, March 14, 2017, http://jmp.princeton.edu /statement.

23. Scott Jaschik, "Hoop Earrings and Hate," *Inside Higher Ed*, March 15, 2017, https://www.insidehighered.com/news/2017/03/15/pitzer-students -debate-free-speech-student-safety-and-cultural-appropriation.

24. American Association of University Professors, "General Report of the Committee on Academic Freedom and Tenure," *Bulletin of the AAUP* 1, no. 1 (December 1915), 32, 36.

25. American Academy of Arts and Sciences, "Charter of Incorporation of the American Academy of Arts and Sciences," n.d., https://www .amacad.org/content/about/about.aspx?d=23.

26. American Academy of Arts and Sciences, "History," n.d., https://www .amacad.org/content.aspx?i=7.

27. Post, "The Classic First Amendment Tradition."

28. Leslie Fiedler, *An End to Innocence: Essays on Culture and Politics* (New York: Stein and Day, 1972), 87.

EPILOGUE

This article and interview were first published in "In the Age of Trump, a Chilling Atmosphere," BillMoyers.com, October 18, 2017, https://billmoyers.com/story/academic-freedom-age-trump/. They later appeared in "In the Trump Age, an Emboldened Attack on Intellectuals," *Salon*, October 23, 2017, https://www.salon.com/2017/10/23/in -the-age-of-trump-a-chilling-atmosphere_partner/.

INDEX

AAC. *See* Association of American Colleges

AAUP. *See* American Association of University Professors

Abu el-Haj, Nadia, 72

academic disciplines: academic freedom in context of, 5, 13, 19–20, 22–24, 33–37, 49, 102–4, 114–15; challenges to, 2, 19, 25–31; as communities, 19, 23–24, 29–32, 49, 102; criticism essential to, 19–20, 26–28, 31, 32–33; dogmatism in, 28, 30; politics of, 49–52; pros and cons of, 5, 19, 23–25, 28, 49–50, 52; standards and rules of, 31–32, 48–49, 102, 143

academic freedom: ambiguities inherent in, 17–19, 23–25, 35, 67–68; attacks on, 2–4, 105; author's experiences with, 15–18, 103, 111, 130–32; central to university's mission, 6–7, 40, 46–47; characteristics and interpretations of, 5–7, 13, 17–25, 39; civility linked to, 70; components of, 6; critical thinking essential to, 2–3, 13–14, 19–20, 41–42, 92–93, 99–101, 108; disciplinary context of, 5, 13, 19–20, 22–24, 33–37, 49, 102–4, 114–15; dogmatism as threat to, 18, 19, 21–22, 24; ethical nature of, 16–17, 19, 35, 37; free speech in relation to, 4, 5–6, 10, 29, 114, 117–18, 121, 135–37; historical conditions of, 17–19; as an ideal, 5–6, 12–13, 15–18; knowledge production linked to, 2–3, 5, 7; as means to common/public good, 14, 119–20, 133–34; origins of, 39–48, 100–101, 119; politics of, 4; in practice, 15–16, 31–37, 48; rationales and defenses for, 7–8, 13–14, 20–22, 99–100, 119; rights vs., 6, 10, 14, 23, 33–34; social inequality in relation to, 12; threats to, 18, 19, 21–22, 24, 93, 143

Previously Published Wellek Library Lectures